AERODRUM

By Nigel Lesmoir-Gordon

Published by Gordon Books

April Cottage,
9, The Green,
Clophill,
Bedfordshire MK45 4AD
UK
© Gordon Books
2013

ISBN

Softcover: 978-0-9573067-6-9

E book: 978-0-9573067-7-6

Gb

www.gordonbooks.co.uk

THIS BOOK IS DEDICATED TO:
Libby
Jody
Bill

ACKNOWLEDGMENTS:
Cover design by Rani Beeri
Front cover photograph by Luke Harmer
Back cover photograph by Gabriel Lesmoir-Gordon

WITH THANKS TO:
Gabriel Lesmoir-Gordon
Sarah Chatwin

PROLOGUE
The Blue Shirt

Two or three times a year in school break times Tibor went to stay with his Uncle Alex and Aunt Vera in Bat Yam, near Tel Aviv for a few days. They had 2 boys Miki and Haim and he always got on very well with them, particularly Miki, who was just a few years younger than Tibor. His Aunt Vera was also from Hungary and had a brother, Shraga, who worked as an engineer at EL-AL Israeli Airline's base in Tel Aviv, Lod International Airport. It's now called Ben Gurion airport.

When Tibor was 14 Shraga picked up on his love of airplanes and he offered to take Tibor to work with him one day. Tibor was most excited by this prospect and really looked forward to the trip. Shraga picked him up from Alex's apartment and they drove up to the airport. Tibor remembers the day vividly - as if it was yesterday. He wore his best shirt - silky dark blue with short sleeves. At the airport they went first to the offices, where Shraga showed

Tibor some of the paperwork connected with his engineering job.

Then Shraga took Tibor out to the hangars. They went into one of them and to Tibor's amazement there was a four-engined Boeing 707, which was being worked on. To the young boy it looked enormous and its beauty completely blew him away. He wondered if this could possibly be the very same aircraft that had flown him into Israel. The 707 was standing on three huge yellow triangular jacks, which suspended it just a few feet off the ground. There were engineers everywhere and Shraga explained to Tibor that it was being weighed, as over time all aircraft have their basic weight re-determined to take into account the many component changes that take place over the years of the life of every aircraft. The aircraft had to be clear of the ground as this was the only way to cycle the landing gear up/down during maintenance.

Shraga asked Tibor if he would like to go into the cockpit with him. He hardly needed to ask. The boy jumped at the opportunity. They climbed up the steep engineering steps. They were steep because the aircraft was much higher than normal off the ground. Once inside the plane they turned left and entered the dimly lit flight deck.

There were labels hanging from the different controls, clearly declaring *Do Not Touch.*

Tibor looked up between the two front seats to the tiny windscreen and asked Shraga why it was so small. He replied that it was only as big as it *needed* to be! He then suggested that Tibor go and sit in the left hand seat - the captain's. Tibor was amazed at the big gap at the front of the seat where it supports the pilot's thighs and asked Shraga what it was for. He explained that it was there to allow the control column to be pulled right back towards the pilot. Wow! Tibor desperately wanted to pull back on the column but dared not touch it. Again there was a notice clearly stating *Do Not Touch.* Like many other airliners of the 60s the 707 was built for a three-man crew. Shraga explained that this third position was for a flight engineer. Tibor didn't want to leave the aircraft. He felt that he could have stayed there forever. That day had a profound and deep impact on him. When he arrived back home he begged his mother never to wash his blue shirt. It had been in touch with a captain's seat. It was a holy relic! The seeds of an exciting life to come had been well and truly sown that day on the 707 flight deck.

Chapter One

Almost Street

Tibor Vásárhelyi was born on 27th September 1954 in Budapest on his father's birthday and because of this he was given the same first name. Tibor. His father was 43 and his mother was 39 when he was born. They had tried for 17 years to have a child so they were overjoyed when he finally appeared in the world.

The family lived in Budapest's 13th precinct in a four storey block of flats constructed in 1941. It was a well-to-do middle class area of the city. The block had three flats on each floor and it was centrally heated with a constant supply of hot water, which was a rare thing in those days. There was a yard in the back where Tibor played with the other children from his own and the neighbouring blocks in the street.

The apartment block they lived in was on Alig Utca and Alig means 'almost'. It was given this name because it was so short. There were 12 blocks in total. The surrounding streets were very similar to Alig – if a bit longer! The blocks of flats in that part of Budapest were all on about four or five floors but each block was highly individual, featuring many different architectural styles.

The apartment block on Alig Street

Alig Street was within walking distance of the Western Train Station. The area was well-served with frequent bus and tram services. The Lehel Food Market with its rich aromas of bread, meat and fish was on the main road at the end of the street. In fact the name Vásárhelyi means 'from a market place'. The market played a big part in Tibor's childhood. He did much of his growing up there. In the evenings he went there to play with his friends when they had the place to themselves. After dark it was their kingdom. They would build dens and push each other around on the wooden trolleys. He has many bright, happy memories of those starlit evenings in that market. The opposite end of Almost Street led down towards the direction of the Danube, that magnificent river, which cut the city in half. His first school was situated on the way down to the river.

Budapest is a beautiful city and Tibor loved it. When he first visited Paris he was struck by the resemblance of that city to Budapest. The same was true of Barcelona, of course, with its Gaudi-fronted apartment blocks and its fine tree-lined avenues.

The flat had one room, a hallway, a kitchenette and a bathroom but no separate lounge. The kitchen was tiny with just enough room to turn round in and it was very much Tibor's mother's kingdom.

Tibor's Aunt Lulu, his father's sister, lived on the third floor in a much bigger flat with a lounge, two bedrooms, two toilets and a small television! Tibor's parents did not have a TV. Lulu and husband József had a daughter called Ágnes and a son László. Tibor and his older cousin Ágnes were very close. In fact, Tibor recalls, they were like one family at times. Ágnes' son Gyuri was just two years younger than Tibor and so they played together a lot. Tibor spent his time between the two flats and they became like one home. He very much enjoyed being upstairs with Gyuri and the TV. They were like brothers growing up together. Although Tibor also enjoyed playing outside on the street, Gyuri did not join him there. Tibor's flat had two windows looking onto the street. The flat upstairs boasted a balcony, which scared Tibor because to him it seemed to be made of very thin material. Even though it had a rail running round, it still looked unsafe and far from the ground. The thought of jumping up and down on it was a terrifying prospect. He did not like to even step out on that balcony and often avoided it.

Ágnes remembers that Tibi, as they called him, was a cheerful little boy with brown wavy hair and brown eyes. She spent a lot of time with him and was always pleased to 'babysit'. She describes the atmosphere in Budapest at that time as 'relaxed'. There was plenty of work and much of the city had been rebuilt following the war.

Central Budapest in the 1950s

Having said that, because Hungary was behind the Iron Curtain, travel to the West was out of the question. There was however a big difference between 1954 when Tibor was born and 1960 following the 1956 uprising, after which many things changed and improved. Even travel to the

West became possible under Prime Minister Kadar János. Ágnes recalls, 'As far as we were concerned the Soviets were welcome after the oppressions of Nazi rule. It felt like Freedom! Since they were a victorious army we accepted their presence and they didn't disturb us.' But Hungary always retained a distinctive personality and its own way of life even though the children were taught Russian at school as their second language.

In 1956 when Tibor was two and with the revolution under way many Hungarians tried to escape and his parents were among them. They packed up everything they could carry and joined up with a group of people to attempt to cross the border by night into Austria. To maintain absolute silence his parents were advised to sedate Tibor for the attempt. It was impossible to cross the border by train so a remote road crossing was chosen. With headlights off the lorry approached the border in silence but Tibor woke and started to wail, just at the wrong time. The lorry was stopped and the passengers were apprehended. They were held in detention overnight in a building that Tibor remembers vividly. He recalls that 'it was like a bathroom with white tiles from floor to ceiling.' As a result of this frightening experience, his parents decided to stay in Hungary and never attempted to escape again.

Tibor and his Father

Tibor's parents both worked. His mother, Róza, had a career in the laboratories at the Number II Children's Hospital in the city. His father held a number of jobs. At the time Tibor's birth he was employed by a transport company, which carried goods throughout Hungary. He managed a depot, which was located next to Tibor's second school.

The walk down to The Danube from Alig Street went past Tibor's first school. Just a minute or two further there was a big playground, St. István Park, where he recalls he spent many happy hours and he cherishes the memory of those times. From the playground he could see the beautiful Margit Island. In summer boats could be boarded to take visitors out to the island. When Tibor was four and his parents were at work along with 20 or so other children he was looked after by a child-carer. Daily she would take the group over to the island. It was a paradise of trees and shrubs and animal enclosures. Some peacocks were allowed to roam free and they enchanted Tibor. He has always been drawn to the countryside. The evocative smell of cut grass has stayed with him and when he catches this scent now it takes him right back to those heady days of his childhood. They took picnics which they ate on benches. There were few trees around Alig Street so these day trips meant a lot to him. The short crossing over The Danube out to the island was always a thrill and he remembers being enchanted by the patterns on the water. On one trip the captain of the ferry invited some children up the wheelhouse. It was an exciting experience especially for Tibor. He recalls that he particularly loved the sound of the enormous diesel engine idling, each and every time they went on board - the rhythm of the tappets and the pistons and the way they repeated and occasionally changed. He feels that this was where some external 'life' noises contained the quality which made him aware of rhythm. It wove itself daily into his subconscious to form the basis from which the art of drumming was to flourish in a big way later in his life.

At around the same age he was sitting at home and listening to music on the radio with a newspaper next to him on the sofa. He picked up a clothes brush with soft black bristles and a wooden handle. He took it in his hand instinctively and started brushing the newspaper in time with the music. His parents noticed and were struck by his connection with the music. It made an impression on them both, one nudging the other pointing towards him. Tibor had no real awareness of what he was doing on those occasions, it was a natural expression. But this connection to the rhythm of the music on the radio was yet another indication of his later enthusiasm for rhythm and drumming.

The Secretary

In his managerial role, his father had a secretary and two years before Tibor was born she became pregnant and gave birth to a daughter, his love child. His father didn't reveal this to Róza immediately but she somehow found out. The secrecy also created a rift and a degree of resentment between her and the family upstairs. She believed that they knew about the child and that they made an effort to keep this knowledge from her. Their motives may have been protective, but she felt let down.

Tibor's Mother and Father

Like little Tibor, his father spent a lot of time upstairs. He enjoyed sharing a beer and watching football and other sports on TV. His mother visited less frequently. Even though they were Jewish the two families always celebrated Christmas. Despite the underlying turbulence, Róza did take part in these family events.

Tibor's half-sister was called Judit. When his mother found out about the child she presented his father with an ultimatum. He had to choose which family he wanted to commit to. His father opted to stay with his wife. She did agree that he could visit his daughter from time to time. Looking back, Tibor gets the impression that his father often took his girl-friend and Judit with him on his frequent business trips. His mother gained some comfort from the fact that she had a *son* and that the girl-friend only had a daughter. Tibor did not find out about his half-sister until many years later. The family upstairs never mentioned this to Tibor. Divorce was a rare event in those days and there was pressure to keep the affair concealed. When Judit was about five she saw photograph of a little boy that fell out of her father's jacket pocket. She picked it up and wanted to know who the little boy was and his father felt compelled to tell her the truth. It puzzles Tibor to this day that his father was honest with Judit and not with him. The truth started to come out one Christmas when Tibor was seven. Tibor and his parents were in the upstairs flat when they heard shouting and screaming on the stairs. It was his father's girl-friend with their daughter and she was demanding to see him because it was Christmas. The adults went out to calm her down and it worked but his transgression was catching up with him. Tibor heard all the noise but protectively no one informed him of its source, or the existence of his nine year old sister.

When Tibor was six he started school. He clearly remembers the Sunday before school began, when he was given his first satchel and how it smelt strongly of leather. He had a sense that he was going to lose some control over his life at school and this feeling brought out a rage, which is an aspect of his character that was going to manifest itself on many occasions throughout his life. It was a trait of his character which perhaps he could well have done without.

However, as it turned out, Tibor enjoyed school. There was nothing special about it but the teaching was good and Tibor learned his lessons well. Earlier, at around the age of four, five he was sent away from home for several weeks to a summer school on the other side of the city in the Buda hills. It was a boarding school and he hated it, even though he went home for the weekends and it was in a very beautiful hilly location with a small swimming pool. Tibor loved this pool and it was the best aspect of the place as far as he was concerned. Tibor hated the food. They often served fish and mushrooms, which were two foods amongst many he could not stand. To get around having to eat the foods he hated, he often secretly stuffed them into the pockets of his shorts and got away with it.

Following a dramatic incident at the summer school he developed a strong aversion to all sea food. At lunch one day, Tibor's neck swelled and he was taken to the childrens' hospital where his mother worked. Luckily for him, he was seen by a doctor who happened to be a close friend of his mother and by whom he always had been treated before. Róza was called and rushed across the hospital to see Tibor. By the time she reached his bedside they had started treatment and the swelling had begun to subside. He had never been in any real danger but the doctor made it clear to Tibor and Róza that he most probably was allergic to sea-food and so should avoid eating fish.

One of the foods he remembers that he loved was strawberries which were always in plentiful supply throughout the summers in Budapest. Aside from the strawberries and the swimming pool there wasn't much else he liked about that time. He did not enjoy sleeping in a mixed dormitory, which he recalls was a big hall with something like 30 beds. He mixed well and was never bullied or singled out for punishment. Yet, when Sunday nights came around his heart would sink at the thought of having to leave home and go back to the school and inevitably his temper broke through. He would scream his displeasure in an attempt to persuade his parents to let him stay at home. It never worked but it established a pattern of throwing temper tantrums when he was unhappy or displeased. Tibor only attended that summer school for three years, but it left him with a challenge to stay calm when he had to do something he didn't want to, or to go somewhere he didn't like. His temper though has never led him to be violent.

Although on the surface his parents appeared to be united and in harmony, looking back Tibor is aware that there was an underlying tension. They didn't row and his father never raised his voice. His mother was more inclined to lose her temper. Tibor was told that on one occasion when his father was travelling on the underground a passenger put a heavy bag on his foot. He said nothing and didn't complain but when the train pulled into the next station he simply picked up the bag and flung it out of the train. Although he was the kind of man who avoided confrontation, he was quite capable of this kind of strong reaction.

Chapter Two

Israel

One fine day in 1962 and quite out of the blue as far as Tibor was concerned Róza announced that she was going to take him to Israel for a month to visit their relatives.

His father would not be going with them. Tibor and his mother had always been close so he was excited about the forthcoming trip.

Tibor and Róza

Róza had two brothers, Alex and Gyula, who both emigrated to Israel, had married and started families there several years before Tibor's visit. At that time Alex had two sons and Gyula had two daughters.

Having taken the train initially to Vienna Róza and Tibor, checked into the Orient Hotel and he was deeply impressed by the building and its Art Nouveau style. Vienna was exciting and so very different from Budapest. In the morning they went out to explore the city and in a small bistro Tibor had his first experience of Coca-Cola. Wow! At this stage the drink had not made its way into Hungary. They visited department stores and in one of them Tibor rode an escalator for the first time in his life.

Then a day or so later they travelled, again by train, through Italy to Naples to take a seven day voyage across the Mediterranean Sea to Israel. They travelled on an overnight train, making one change on the way. Tibor woke in the middle of the night to discover that the compartment they had gone to sleep in on their own had been invaded by four Italians. Tibor was terrified. He couldn't figure out who these people were. Their language was completely foreign to him too. He had wrongly assumed that the compartment was theirs and was exclusive to them.

Naples welcomed them with warm, bright sunshine. They checked into their hotel, put their luggage in their room and went out to eat. They found a restaurant right next to the hotel with tables outside on the pavement. As they were sitting down Tibor spotted a huge plate of snails being served to a couple at the next table. His reaction was immediate. He threw up. This strong response was probably caused by a combination of the heat, the sight and smell of the snails.

This was the first time that Tibor saw the sea. Hungary is a land-locked country and as result he had never had this experience before. Róza took Tibor to an office on the quay to pick up the pre-arranged tickets for the voyage. The agent asked his mother to go with him to another office and Tibor was left on his own to wait there. Although there were a few people around after ten minutes he understandably became anxious and started to cry. He felt out of his depth and abandoned amongst these foreign office people. Fortunately Róza returned soon after with their tickets for the following day on a Turkish ship called The Istanbul, which carried both passengers and cargo.

As they climbed aboard Tibor was struck by the enormous cranes on the deck. They impressed him as did the smell of diesel, which reminded him of his ferry trips across The Danube. It was another very exciting world and Tibor loved it immediately. This time they had a cabin to themselves and there were no interruptions in the middle of the night. As soon as they sailed Tibor went up on deck. He loved the sea and standing at the bows watching the waves part beneath him. For a child who had never seen the sea before this was stunning. Wherever he looked it was endless sea and sky and it was deeply satisfying. He loved the warmth and the continuous sunshine. It was paradise. There were evening entertainments including a band playing tangos and people dancing. The food was good too. Tibor spent his time up on deck and Róza read books and did crossword puzzles. It was the same when they went on holidays in Hungary. Róza did crosswords. On the ship Tibor recalls that his mother completed 'thousands and thousands of crosswords'.

Then one day at dawn Róza woke him, took him straight up on deck to show him the distant flickering lights of the first bit of land that they had seen for 7 days. They were looking at the approaching port of Haifa. Even though they were still a fair way off the coast, they could see the city and the outline of Mount Carmel behind it. This was a sight he has never forgotten. It made a deep and lasting impression on him. When they docked Tibor was immediately struck by the enormous, dominating processing building for passengers.

Initially they stayed with Gyula and his family in Haifa. Tibor got to know his two cousins well and enjoyed their company. Having two girl cousins was something new and very special to him. Róza was over-the-moon to be with her brother again after several years of being apart. Tibor loved the Mediterranean food - the salads and the humus, the falafels - so different from what they ate at home in Hungary. The family lived in a top floor flat of a four story apartment building. The children spent a lot of time on the balcony and in the gardens between the blocks. He made many other friends amongst the children there as he slowly learnt what it was like to live in another country. Tibor has very fond memories of that time in Haifa.

After two weeks or so they moved on to Jaffa to stay with Alex, his wife Vera and their children. They lived in a very old building on the beach, which Tibor felt must surely be due to be demolished. Their balcony was a roof terrace, which overlooked the sea. It was a very different setting to the apartment in Haifa. Alex had two sons at this stage, one with Vera whose name was Miki. Gabriel, the older one was living by then with his mother, Kati, in the

USA. She was Vera's sister and Alex's first wife. As it happened Gabriel, or Gabi as he was known, was visiting his father and younger brother Miki at the time of Tibor's visit. They spent many happy hours playing together in the sunshine on the balcony and on the nearby beach. Tibor loved the climate and the company and felt no desire at all to go home to Budapest.

The camel, Aunt Vera and Tibor

Tibor has a very clear memory of riding a camel on a day out with his Aunt Vera. It was a frightening experience. He was placed on a saddle between the camel's two humps. He was taken by surprise when the camel straightened its back legs hurling Tibor forward at a mad angle but he clung on until the camel straightened its front legs. Eventually he was calm enough to take a short ride but was greatly relieved to get his feet back on solid ground.

Tibor was sad when the time came for them to set off for Hungary. They sailed back to Naples on the Istanbul's sister ship, the Adana. They left Haifa in the middle of a storm and it was very rough. Tibor enjoyed being thrown about by the turbulent waves, unlike on the back of that camel (a ship of the desert!). Many of the passengers were frightened but Tibor had full faith in the ship. It was thrilling and wild. After seven days they arrived back in Naples safe and sound and caught the train to Budapest, reaching the city just a few days after the start of the school year in September.

Chapter Three
Back in Budapest

There was a shock in store for Tibor and Róza at Budapest's Western Railway Station. His father was waiting for them. When he and his mother climbed down from the train and Tibor caught sight of his father, the first thing he noticed was his father's shoes, both of which had a section of the upper sole missing. Tibor could see his socks. Nothing was explained to Tibor at the time and the family went home.

Although he was aware that his father had circulatory problems, until then he looked and behaved like a healthy 50 year old man. This was the first sign that something was seriously wrong.

Soon after this his father's health deteriorated and he was unable to work. Róza carried on working and Tibor had to help with his father's lunch. In Hungary at that time there were many take-away food services being run privately from flats in the city. When school lunch breaks came around, Tibor walked to a specific address and collected a metal food carrier which contained three separate pots. He took the food carrier back to their flat and delivered the hot meal to his father. He could see that he was in absolute agony, in particular around his stomach. Tibor had never seen him like this before - in pain and showing it. He was a proud man so it was obvious to Tibor that his father was suffering.

Some time later Tibor was told that his father had a narrowing of the arteries and that blood was not getting properly to his feet, causing a lot of discomfort, which is why he'd cut away parts of his shoes, partly easing the pain. As it turned out his father had also been diagnosed with pancreatic cancer and it was spreading. He was hospitalized and told that as a result of blocked arteries both his legs would be amputated - all this at the age of just 51.

One Sunday afternoon his mother took Tibor to visit his father in hospital in Buda - the finest and most elegant part of the city. He looked ok to Tibor and they spent an hour or so with him. Next day after Tibor finished the morning session at school he went home and arrived at about two in the afternoon. So he was very surprised to find that his mother was there and wondered why. Róza made no effort to explain, but she looked very unhappy. Then Tibor spotted his father's suitcase leaning against the wall in the hallway. He knew that his father had taken that same case to the hospital with him and the truth started to dawn on him. He looked hard at Róza and asked her why the suitcase was back there in the flat. His mother was lost for words and Tibor came right out and asked, 'He's not dead, is he?' She prevaricated but eventually broke down in tears saying, 'Yes he is,' and they cried together. It transpired that his father had refused to have his legs amputated and in a strange way Tibor was pleased that this operation had not gone ahead and that his father had died physically intact.

Tibor was only 10 and now had to face life without his father. He felt the loss acutely. However, a short time later he decided to go out to play and chose to visit a friend at the end of the street. Play got a bit noisy which prompted the friend's mother to come in to the room. She confronted Tibor and asked him "How could you possibly think about playing when your father had just died?" Tibor was lost for words and was surprised by this insensitive abruptness. Looking back he considers her remarks inappropriate for such a young child. He feels now that she should have appreciated that he needed to take his mind off his loss, given that he could not bring his father back however much he tried. Life had to go on.

Tibor did not go to his father's funeral. The reason for this became clear to him later but at the time nothing was explained to him. It was deeply puzzling to the young boy. The reason he was not taken to the funeral was in fact because the family felt that his father's mistress might turn up, cause a scene and then all would be revealed to Tibor.

Given that he was just 10 years old when his father passed away, looking back he has understandably few vivid memories of his father. He can recall however, that he had a bicycle with stabilizers. It was safe for the children to play in the street. It was like things were in England in days gone by, which Tibor has seen in photographs taken in cities like Liverpool and Manchester in the middle of the last century. One day while he was playing in the street with friends his father came out and removed the stabilizers from the bicycle. He took a broomstick, which he fixed on the back of the bike vertically behind the saddle. He pushed Tibor off and ran behind him steadying the boy and holding him upright with the broomstick, hoping that before he ran out of energy, the boy would master the balancing act himself. After numerous runs up and down the street his father let him go and Tibor was away, holding himself upright and balancing perfectly.

There was a day Tibor spent with his father that he remembers well. There is a bridge linking Buda and Pest, which touches the southern tip of Margit Island. As Tibor recalls the Danube completely freezes over in winter and the bridge is the only way to get onto the island. There were obviously no ferry sailings. Margit Bridge was part of the route to be taken by the visiting Russian leader Nikita Khrushchev's motorcade and it was crowded with people to see him pass by. The city put on a spectacular air display for Khrushchev. Several low-flying aircraft each towing a glider flew over the bridge. Tibor remembers that the planes flew so low he could actually see the faces of the pilots sitting in the aircraft. It was thrilling and made a big impression on Tibor, sowing more seeds for the career he would eventually follow. There was also a spectacular parachuting display, which he enjoyed enormously.

The Danube and Margit Island with Margit bridge at the far end

On some Sunday mornings Tibor and his father caught a bus into the city to visit the beautiful and elegant art deco Café Gerbeaud where they bought the most amazing desserts at the takeaway counter. An incredibly strong smell of coffee and cakes greeted the visitor. There were rattan chairs, awesome chandeliers and different coloured rooms, which Tibor liked to explore while his father chose the desserts for the day. Róza always cooked a special meal on Sundays and these desserts were a fitting complement. On some other Sundays, they went to different restaurants for lunch, occasionally in the open air. The sound of clinking cutlery has always brought back fond memories of these rich family moments.

Looking back it's unclear to Tibor just how well off the family were. He can see that they did not have a great deal of money, but weren't so short that they couldn't afford to buy him toys, although he often had to press hard for expensive things like proper Canadian Hockey ice skates. Given that they lived in a one room apartment it is clear that they had to live on a fairly tight budget.

Róza and his father were both very hard working. Although Tibor senior did not go to university, or hold any special qualifications, he was able enough to have a managerial post at a large and thriving transport company, where he had a lot of responsibility. Róza's job in the hospital required that she sat and passed a series of demanding examinations. It was a professional post and she was well respected.

The family could also afford to take regular summer holidays in the countryside outside Budapest. Tibor enjoyed these times enormously. On one occasion, he and his Mother went to stay on the shores of Lake Balaton, which is a freshwater lake in the Transdanubian region of Hungary. It is in fact the largest lake in Central Europe. Tibor remembers a particular day when he joined a group of children splashing around on an inflatable mattress. They were playing happily until the weather changed abruptly sending large waves crashing onto the shore. One of these waves flipped the mattress over spilling the children into the water. Although he wasn't aware of it, Tibor's foot was caught in between some wooden steps leading down into the water. Looking back it was a very odd experience. Strangely he stayed calm even though he was completely submerged, not breathing. He didn't struggle and was relaxed even when he started to have coloured flashes in his head. Róza saw that when the children clambered back on shore Tibor was not among them. She panicked and ran screaming up and down the beach searching for him. Fortunately one of the holiday-makers spotted his foot and they managed to pull him out. He was pretty far gone but putting pressure on his chest they forced the water out of his lungs and Tibor remembers suddenly coming to himself when the water gushed out of him and he started coughing and then breathing again. Notably Tibor was not frightened by this experience and has maintained his love of water and swimming. Now he swims twice a week.

When Tibor was eight years old he fell in love with ice skating. Heroes Square is in the centre of Budapest. Its iconic statue complex, the Millennium Memorial, was completed in 1900. It's was vast and impressive open space where they held big parades in those days similar to those that took place in front of The Kremlin in Moscow. Behind the square there was a boating lake, which was artificial but looked natural and Tibor found it very enchanting. In winter the lake was frozen by a system of cooling pipes running underneath it, creating a impressively large skating rink. Tibor went there often with a couple of girls he knew. Marika and Ágnes F both attended the same school as Tibor. They took the trolley bus to Heroes Square. It was a twenty minute ride and they would skate there for a couple of hours. Even though he was only 11, Tibor developed an emotional attachment to Ágnes F. He found her very beautiful and attractive. She had blonde hair down to her shoulder with one side tucked behind her ear. He thought she was striking and very sexy. One day after school they were standing on the school corner on the way home and Tibor found himself expressing his feelings for her. Ágnes F's reaction was immediate and crushing. Its vehemence took Tibor by surprise. She exclaimed: 'I hate you like shit!' It was a real smack in the face for him and it surprised him because he knew she liked him. Nonetheless they carried on skating together. A week or so later the three of them were changing out of their skates when Marika turned to Tibor and told him that Ágnes F wanted to kiss him. Girls, thought Tibor! In the event they didn't kiss, he felt it was too public and he was too shy.

The Sister

One day after school sometime after his father's death something very powerful and significant occurred in his life. He was at home alone and there was a knock on the door. He half opened the door and found a girl standing there, who he had never seen before. She asked his name and he confirmed that it was Tibor. She asked him to follow her downstairs to meet another girl who wanted to talk to him. Outside on the street the other girl was waiting for them and she, having made sure who he was, announced without preamble or ceremony that she was his sister, Judit. Tibor was taken aback. He looked hard at her and declared immediately that he did not have a sister and that was that. He didn't stay on the street but went straight back upstairs, putting the incident out of his mind. However sometime later he mentioned the event in passing to his mother. She stopped right there in her tracks. She looked like she was going to lose her temper. But she managed to maintain her composure and insisted that he did not have a sister. End of story or so Róza thought.

He quickly forgot the incident until a letter arrived for him. It was from Judit in which she repeated that she was his sister and that he should speak to his mother about her. Tibor gave the letter to Róza. She became furious but not with Tibor. She realized then that she had to be truthful with her son. She admitted that he *did* have a half-sister, but insisted that he should not see her again, or attempt to contact her. It seemed more important for her to keep this segregation between her son and his half sister, rather than allow some kind of relationship to develop between the two of them. It would have been too painful and a constant reminder of the difficult past.

Tibor agreed to this. Strangely he didn't feel any need to dig deeper into the matter. Looking back now Tibor is surprised that he could let the subject rest and forget about it so easily. He simply did not have a need to find out more. He would not hear from Judit again for many years.

Without her husband Róza felt lonely and isolated. She had very little contact with the family upstairs and few friends in the area. Her relatives were all in Israel. Over the next months she found herself reflecting more and more on the horrors of World War II. For instance the time when she had to go into hiding from the Germans, or having to carry false identification and the not knowing of what happened to her husband when he was forced to go to a work camp.

She slowly came to the conclusion that Israel would be a far better and safer place for them to live as well as bringing her closer to her brothers and their families. So she began preparations for applying for them to emigrate. At that time emigration was almost unheard of but she was determined. She explained her intention to Tibor and he was thrilled not least because she planned that they would travel by air.

In the course of her efforts to set the process in motion Róza established good connections with some of the officials in the civil service. She came to an arrangement that the flat they rented would be signed over to one of the officials in return for processing their visas and the other formalities. This was common practice in Hungary at that time. It was the way things worked. Eventually they had the clearance to leave and that same official did indeed take on the rental of their flat.

In the weeks leading up to their departure in June 1967 Róza packed all their possessions in tea chests and arranged for a haulage company to come and collect them for shipment to Israel. With their furniture gone they slept on lilos with the minimum of home amenities. The flat was virtually an empty shell. Tibor continued to attend school. Not long after their possessions left and they were about to leave Budapest it was announced on the news that war had broken out in the Middle East. Róza was convinced that she had made a terrible mistake and her world fell apart. But fortunately for them the war known as the Six Day War was over in just six days! Within that short period, Israel had won a decisive land war. Israeli forces had taken control of the Gaza Strip and the Sinai Peninsula from Egypt, the West Bank and East Jerusalem from Jordan, and the Golan Heights from Syria. An uneasy peace returned to the region just one week before their planned departure and their travel plans once more swung into action. They didn't have to change their itinerary. What a relief it was for both of them! It was as if nothing had happened.

Tibor will never forget the day they left. Looking back he sees that it was probably the most exciting day in his life. However there were no big goodbyes with the family upstairs when they left Budapest. Róza continued to resent the fact that they had kept her in the dark with regard to his father's affair and the fact that he had a daughter.

Malév Ilyushin IL-18

They travelled out to Budapest airport in the evening.

The first leg of the journey was a one hour flight to Athens. The aircraft was a Russian four-engined Ilyushin Il-18. The night was clear and even though the aircraft was old it was hugely exciting for Tibor to be actually flying. They sat on the right hand side and when the plane banked Tibor could see the whole of Budapest laid out below him, all lit up. It was a truly amazing and thrilling sight for the young boy.

Chapter Four

A New Life in Israel

Having arrived in Athens, they had to wait a couple of days to meet up with an Israeli agent, who would give them their El-Al tickets for the flight to Tel Aviv. Their hotel room overlooked a girls' school. One morning Tibor was standing on the balcony and he remembers the girls in the classroom opposite pointing at him and laughing for no apparent reason but there was no time to go out or make friends.

Eventually the agent arrived. He was strikingly tall with cropped hair, giving Tibor his first experience of the Israeli security forces. Tibor sat on the balcony while Róza went through the formal arrangements, which had to be handled in person, in connection with their flight and arrival in Tel Aviv.

They were to fly in a Boeing 707 - a big, long, four-engined passenger jet. He loved the shape of the round fuselage and the engines. This was a huge thrill for Tibor. Thinking back he can safely say that it was the sexiest thing in the world that he could possibly have imagined. They sat on the left of the aircraft and unlike on the previous Ilyushin flight, he remembers during take-off being pressed deep into his seat and it left a very vivid impression on him - further seeds of what was to come. The 707 flew at 600 mph and they were swiftly transported to Tel Aviv and their new life.

They landed mid-evening and took a room at a hotel by the airport. Tibor was struck again by the incredible heat and it dawned on him that they had indeed moved to a very hot country. Tibor was able to cope. For his mother it wasn't so easy. Early the following morning his two uncles, Alex and Gyula came to meet them. Róza was over-the-moon to see them both again. To start with, they stayed with Gyula in Haifa while they waited for their own flat to be arranged. As immigrants they were entitled to free accommodation and after a few weeks they moved into a newly built apartment, which was just fifteen minutes walk from his uncle's apartment block towards the foothills of Mount Carmel. Their apartment's balcony looked out towards this impressive mountain, which dominates the city. There was a small playground behind the apartments that led up to a main road and which went right up to the top of the mountain.

The pleasant flat was new and smelt fresh and unlived in. But there was one problem as far as Róza was concerned. The flat was on the top floor. There was no lift and they had to climb 165 steps to reach their apartment. Ascending the stairs left her breathless and she wasn't happy about this. Although air-conditioning was fairly common-place at that time, their flat did not have it. There is little rain in Israel and the roof of the block was flat, which increased the heat inside their top floor apartment. As a result it could become very uncomfortable indeed but they did their best to get used to it.

Róza very soon started taking classes in Hebrew in a local community centre. She needed to master the language of course, before she could get a job. She aspired to work in Haifa's largest hospital, Rambam. The language is not easy to learn with its unique characters. Unlike Hungarian the writing flows from right to left. Tibor used to sit in on the classes unofficially, as he was keen to learn the language too.

Then diplomatic relations between Hungary and Israel soured and contact was severed for a time. Ágnes remembers sadly how she lost touch with Tibor in those years. She regrets that she didn't see him throughout his teens. She would have enjoyed being a part of his growing up and to have shared that with him.

Tibor was nearly 12 and it was essential for him to start school again and learn Hebrew. His aunt suggested that he attend an agricultural boarding school for immigrants called Meir Shfeya, which she had found, in a very beautiful location about half an hour by bus from Haifa.

Most of the other pupils in his dormitory were from French speaking Morocco. They continued to speak French among themselves and as a result Tibor started to pick up French first, rather than Hebrew. Having said that there were several Israeli children at the school and all the classes were conducted in Hebrew so he slowly but surely began to pick up the language. Interestingly for him, there was one other Hungarian at the school, which was comforting and reassuring although strangely Tibor didn't really take to this boy. He found him a little weird and so avoided him.

Tibor stayed at the school for one year. He didn't like boarding away from home and made it clear to his mother and his uncle's family that he wanted to move on. They found him a place in a school about five minutes walk from their apartment.

Tibor the schoolboy

The first pupil he made contact with there was an Israeli born boy called Dani Shmuely, from a Hungarian background and they immediately became friends. He also noticed a very pretty girl in his class. After they met on the very first day of school, Dani invited Tibor to visit his home where they spoke Hungarian. He had only been there for a couple of minutes when in walked this same girl. As it turned out she was Dani's twin sister, Dorit. What a surprise! Their parents spoke Hungarian to each other, but addressed the twins in both languages, Hebrew and Hungarian. Even though he spoke Hungarian at home it was a joy to be in another household where they did the same. Tibor was rapidly gaining command of Hebrew, which he actually found easy to learn. His confidence grew with his mastering the language. Tibor liked Dani and his father Imre too. He found him friendly and amusing. Tibor spent a lot of time with the family and became very close to them.

Tibor only attended that school for a year when his age dictated that he move on. He recalls that he was exempted from the end of year exams because he had started late. As it happened he was given a pass anyway, so that he progressed to the next level in his education without him being left behind.

In 1968 he chose another boarding school, which was surprising given that he did not enjoy being away from home. This school was again located about half an hour's bus ride from where he lived, in an industrial area on the outskirts of Haifa. It was on a large Air Force base, taking in children who were keen on aviation. Tibor was already starting to take an interest in flying. He was at the school from Monday to Friday, returning home for the weekends. The pupils were encouraged to explore the base, which Tibor really enjoyed. Outside the school was a Meteor - a vintage twin-engined jet. The plane was not in good condition but Tibor loved just to look at it. Unfortunately the pupils were never allowed to sit in the cockpit. There was some air traffic in and out of the base and Tibor liked watching the planes whenever he could.

He had some difficulties with his studies, particularly mathematics. His teacher knew his stuff but had great difficulty teaching it to his students and Tibor was left behind. He did well however with engineering particularly when he studied radial piston aircraft engines. He soon learnt how this kind of technology worked.

One day the school organized a visit by the Israeli performer Uri Geller. He was not yet well-known at the time, but his performance knocked them all sideways. Geller talked about telekinesis and telepathy. He asked some of the students to write down numbers, put them into sealed envelopes, which he later correctly ascertained. Tibor was convinced that there was no cheating involved because Geller knew none of the pupils. He bent spoons and drove a car round the school yard blindfold. They all loved his demonstrations and were very impressed. Later of course he became world famous.

Some evenings Tibor and his friends crawled through a gap in the fence and went home. They would always be back in the morning in time for school. Occasionally Tibor went alone. Looking back Tibor is aware that had they been older they would have gone into town, but going home was good enough for him. It was always an adventure even if they did sometimes get caught. Given that the school authorities were responsible for their safety, they treated the escapees very leniently.

Tibor completed his first year at that school without attaining any particular distinction. He decided that the school did not in fact focus enough on aviation and left at the year's end.

At around this time Róza got a very good job at the Rambam Hospital in the Bat-Galim neighbourhood of Haifa. It was the largest medical centre in northern Israel and the fifth largest in Israel. It was named after the 12th century physician-philosopher Rabbi Moshe Ben-Maimon (Maimonides). She did exactly the same kind of work she had done in Budapest. Her Hebrew had come on in leaps and bounds and she was proficient enough to hold down the job. She dealt with the samples that came into the laboratory, using centrifuges and auto-analysers. She loved the work and had a good salary - enough for them to live comfortably. Shortly after, Tibor left the boarding school and as a result of Róza's efforts they managed to move to another nearby apartment. Their flat was on the first floor in an older building. It had one main bedroom and they converted the dining room into a bedroom for Tibor, with glass doors. It had a lounge with a balcony, a utility room and a kitchen, which also featured a small balcony looking out over Mount Carmel. Above them on the hillside there were other blocks of flats. Unlike their first flat there was a partial view of the sea, which was about four or five miles distant.

Although they left it a bit late Tibor was able to find a place in another school where he stayed for the last three years of his education. This school was funded by the Electricity Board and it was aimed at training pupils to be electricians. It was a fair distance from where they lived and required that Tibor took two buses. One particular advantage at that school was that they taught some English language, which would come in very useful later on in his life. He took to English immediately and he was the best student in his class in this subject. It was then at the age of 14 that Tibor became aware of Western popular music. He was walking down the road one day when he heard the sound of Jimi Hendrix pouring out of an open window. 'What is that?' he wondered. It struck him powerfully and created a strong reaction in him and he knew he had to find out more. He felt a deep *need* to get involved. He heard Deep Purple with the drumming of Ian Pace (who later makes an appearance in the story), which is what *really* grabbed his attention. He realized there and then that he wanted to be a drummer and that he must learn to play somehow. Everything else faded into the background. That feeling he had as a very young child with the newspaper and the brush came flooding back to him. In desperation, he found solace in drawing different arrangements of drum kits on endless pieces of paper, particularly during school lessons. That is when he wasn't drawing large passenger jets! At home he covered the walls with publicity shots of amazing looking drums from magazines. Around this time he created a makeshift 'kit': a hi-hat made out of two ends of large olive tins, joined in the centre with a bent nail, adding other objects, spreading them out on his bed. Then with a couple of drum sticks he was 'playing along' to music he liked. Not to mention copious amounts of air-drumming, playing in time to music, imagining himself in a band watched by huge crowds. He then went on to discover Yes, Genesis, Pink Floyd, Led Zeppelin, Deep Purple, Rush, ACDC, Grand Funk Railroad, Ursa Major and the rest. His most favourite drummer of all time is Alan White of Yes, followed closely by Phil Collins, Ian Pace of Deep Purple and Neil Peart from Rush.

Chapter Five

The Band

Tibor told Róza that more than anything in the world he wanted a drum kit. He couldn't afford to buy one. Nor could she. She said that if he wanted drums he would have to work for them so he took a part-time job in a biscuit factory downtown. He hated every minute of it and was never going to save enough to buy a drum kit. In the event he was sacked for irregular attendance. At this point his Uncle Alex came into the picture in a big way. Alex was a tourist guide and he drove a very smart seven-seater Mercedes. Every year he was given a subsidy to buy a new car by the tourist board to drive well off visitors around the country. Occasionally his work brought him to Haifa and he would visit the family. On one of these visits Tibor declared his strong desire for a drum kit and asked his uncle for his help. As it happened, in the 50s Alex had been a drummer himself in Hungary many years before he immigrated to Israel. Tibor can't recall the details but somehow his uncle and mother managed to raise enough money to eventually buy him a drum kit. One evening they drove up Mount Carmel to collect the equipment, which Alex had sourced. Although it was really old, it was a truly wonderful thing for Tibor to have his own kit.

The first kit

By this time Tibor had started to go out at night with friends to see bands perform. Because it was so warm there was no need for a venue. Bands could perform in the open air. A particularly favoured location was in a huge gothic style gateway in the grounds of the University of Haifa up on the Carmel. One particular band stands out in his memory, Beber and The Souls. They were playing American and British covers with no original material but they were very good musicians. The band looked and sounded great. Tibor and his friends were star-struck to say the least. The lead singer reminded them of Mick Jagger and they just gawped. Tibor of course didn't watch the singer so much as the drummer, David Almishali because watching and copying was going to be his way to learn and then master the art of drumming. He knew he had a lot to take in and he was ready to put in the effort. With his own drum kit he started to study and memorise the techniques of drummers in the bands he went to see. Occasionally at home he practiced without any background music, sometimes very much with. He was very dedicated and knew he had the necessary coordination. It didn't take Tibor long to realise that he had chosen the right instrument and his confidence started to grow rapidly.

One day he got into conversation with a guy of about his own age, who told him that there was a very talented singer/guitarist called Shimon Holly, who lived in a nearby village. It was suggested that they should meet up and by arrangement this took place one day. They discovered their passion for the same kind of music and started rehearsing together. Shimon suggested that they find a bass player and try to get a gig. He started to look for a place for their first performance in public. Tibor was worried. His drum kit wasn't really fit to play at a live gig. He had no drum stool just a combination of a wooden chair, topped off with a wooden foldable chess board and a blanket, but it was the right height. The drums too were sadly lacking. They had animal skins unlike today's modern plastic equivalent. But Tibor put his fears and doubts aside. He was up for it!

Although they had never rehearsed together the bass player Shimon had found was also ready to give it a go. He was a couple of years older than Tibor and Shimon and was something of a father-figure to them both. He had some experience and had played with several other bands. He wasn't lacking in confidence either. He was Yossi Lang.

Tibor drumming with his later band, featuring Benjo and Beber

Tibor remembers their first gig vividly. With so little rehearsal and never having actually played as a trio it was terrifying and he felt in a way like he was sleep-walking. But there was Yossi the bass player on his left and there was Shimon on his right. It was happening and they gave it their all.

It was a medium sized venue, but it had a stage and they drew a satisfyingly large crowd. Tibor did have some tricky technical problems to contend with. His bass drum kept slipping away from him and he's certainly not the only drummer in the world to have had to deal with this issue. To get round this set-back he learned to improvise after this first gig. He found that if he ran some string out from the drum and tied the other end to a chair it helped to keep the drum where he wanted it!

The trio had several more gigs. Yossi played with other bands but he fitted in well with Tibor and Shimon and wanted to play with them as often as he could. Eventually he got a permanent post as bass player with the resident band at one of the most prestigious clubs, The Haifa Theatre Club. It was a good job. Many international artists performed at the club. Tibor recalls hearing Madeline Bell sing there one night.

Then Benjo joined the band to play bass, replacing Yossi. Tibor liked him and they finally started to rehearse as a trio. Both Shimon and Benjo came from an Egyptian, Jewish background, mixing nicely with the Hungarian TNT! Their passion for music bonded them together, notwithstanding the - unplanned at this stage - addition from a Moroccan origin.

Tibor was learning and improving fast. He cannot recall anyone being critical of his drumming, instead receiving a lot of praise after the gigs, from other musicians as well. The band was well-received and their efforts were appreciated by the crowds. His confidence continued to grow.

Then the area's most respected and famous person, Beber, joined the band as lead singer and they became a foursome. They had a new name 'Bereshit' but they were far from being shit. That's just a sad consequence of translation! Bereshit in Hebrew is the first word in the Old Testament meaning *'In the beginning'*. They became very well known and were sought after at weekends.

Things were looking up. Two years makes a big difference to teenagers and, even though Benjo at 19 was also older than Tibor and Shimon, audiences were impressed by their youth and their enthusiasm.

Interest in the band started to increase exponentially as their reputation spread throughout Israel and they started to be in demand far and wide, often having to travel north and south to venues as much as three hours distance from home. Beber and Benjo had to hold down day jobs. Tibor and Shimon were still at school. Education took a back seat as far as Tibor was concerned. They were soon offered opportunities to play at open air festivals and they entered many competitions, which they often won.

They won at Yavne in 1973. Shimon is first on the left

Drumming was by far and away Tibor's greatest love. This was what he wanted and what he was *meant* to do.

This was it and there was no stopping him. They played at the end of year concert at school and his street cred went through the roof. Playing in front of his mates was really gratifying and it made him feel good about himself. A full circle from those air-drumming, bed bashing days at home - alone!

The band started to smoke hashish, which was readily available and cheap. The drug seemed well-suited to their music and their image. They enjoyed getting stoned and did so quite often. Naturally one thing led to another and they also experimented with other drugs. The band was scheduled to play at a gig on the outskirts of Haifa. As usual they met at the Moulin Rouge Café where Tibor and Shimon picked up two stamps, which were impregnated with LSD, from a guy they knew. He instructed them to lick the stamps and wait for the effect to kick in. Very soon, he explained, they would start to feel weird! They climbed into the van and licked the stamps without a second thought. Nothing much happened. They arrived at the venue, unloaded and started to set up their gear. Tibor managed to set up his drum kit without any difficulties. A little later, he caught site of Shimon, who was standing in the still empty hall. The moment they eyes met they burst into uncontrollable laughter, which went on and on - much longer than normal. They knew then that they were 'getting it'. Tibor recalls that the sensation was wonderful and not at all unpleasant. The band completed their sound check and waited for their audience to arrive. It was only when they started to play that Tibor's problems began. Initially he had issues with his timing, which is not at all ideal if you're playing with a band, you're the drummer and you are live! He started to get some very strange looks from the bass player and the singer. Tibor couldn't figure out what was going on and what he was doing wrong. He simply couldn't work out if he was playing too slowly or too fast. As far as Tibor could tell Shimon was alright and playing well, which gave Tibor some confidence to carry on and keep trying.

Other stranger and difficult problems started to beset Tibor. At one point it seemed to him that his drum sticks were no longer straight but were curving upwards, describing a half circle. Consequently Tibor felt he had to hit the drums and cymbals at an odd angle and the band were starting to react and look more worried. The audience too was responding in an alarming way. Whenever he looked out over the crowd they seemed to be looking at

him with demonic disapproval. They looked disappointed.
The coloured lights spilling over the band did nothing to
lessen the growing onslaught of the LSD and Tibor was
feeling more and more paranoid. He couldn't follow the
music or even keep close to the beat. Everything was falling
apart rapidly. Eventually he had to give up. He downed his
sticks and walked straight off the stage without looking
back. He was running scared. Very scared! The only safe
place he could think of right then was their van and he
headed straight for it. He managed to open the rear door
and he clambered in, slamming it behind him.

The band was forced to take a break. Shimon told the
rest that they had taken LSD. They then followed Tibor into
the van. Beber was not by nature a patient man, but he
weighed up the situation and made a decision not to come
down heavily on Tibor. He was not into getting high so
there was no way he could have understood fully what
Tibor was feeling and going through. However he was able
to stay calm and slowly explained to Tibor that he had
caused a big disturbance at the gig. The audience was
disappointed and some people were starting to get angry.
The venue management was very unhappy with the
situation too. Beber told Tibor that he should have known

better and insisted that he go back inside and finish the gig. Tibor responded that he couldn't cope with this. He had no control over his body or his mind and he couldn't understand what was going on or how to handle anything, let alone playing his drums on stage. The band were determined and gently worked on persuading him to go back in. They assured him that he was an excellent drummer, that he always played well and that it was essential that he did his best to finish the job.

Full of fear and trepidation Tibor went back onstage. Most of the rest of that gig remains a blur in his memory but he can recall that later on, as if in a film, he found himself sitting on his stool backwards, facing the wall, with the kit behind him, under the intense bright lighting. No one from the band was talking to him at that stage, the audience had gone and the band was in the process of packing up their equipment. At least it was over and Tibor is amazed to this day that he managed to finish the gig. Or did he?

Tibor remembers being dropped off back home later on that night. They helped him get his drum kit back into the flat and then left. Róza was sleeping and they worked quietly to avoid waking her. She was used to Tibor coming home with his kit late at night and she was a good sleeper. Tibor went to his bedroom and crept into bed, hoping to sleep off the nightmare. This was a big mistake! Sleep was out of the question! His mind had changed gear and the experience intensified. He stared out of his bedroom window into the darkness and watched a tree that swayed to and fro in the breeze looking quite threatening. Tibor didn't have the experience or the knowledge to deal with the effects of the mind-bending drug. It was so much stronger than anything he had ever taken before. It was bigger than him and he was unable to steer himself out of the nightmare. He knew then what it was like to be mad. More than anything he wanted the old Tibor back and the more he wanted this the worse it became. He was scared by everything - every thought, every sight, every sound. Added to this he was scared that his mother would realise what he had done.

As the night wore on things became totally unbearable. Tibor got up and went in search of help and some safety. He went into Róza's bedroom and woke her. He did the very thing that he had been fearing most of all but he was desperate. He hoped that because she was not on the drug herself, she might be his *only* way of being helped back to sanity! Róza got up and realized immediately that Tibor was in a terrible state. She led him to the kitchen and made a hot drink for both of them while he explained that he and Shimon had taken a drug that made him feel that he had completely lost touch with reality and his sanity. Her reaction was totally unexpected. Instead of being angry with him she was soft and gentle. She talked to him and did her best to calm him. Looking back, Tibor feels that somehow she picked up on his state and really understood what he was going through. As it turned out Róza was the best person that he could have turned to. If he had tried to hide the truth his agony would have only increased and she would have found out somehow. He started to relax and slow down. She stayed with him until he became calmer. He was so grateful for her help, understanding and support. Eventually he went back to bed and slept. The storm passed and Tibor slowly regained his sanity.

Although Tibor and the band were into heavy rock, he got to know many other musicians with very different tastes in the scene around Haifa. He recalls one particular superb vocalist, who made an impression on him. Rafi wasn't very much into heavy rock, but appreciated Tibor's ability and they became friends. They lived pretty close to each other, so popping around was easy. He had a regular job with a band that had residency in a weddings venue. Rafi occasionally offered him work. Tibor managed to adapt himself to the kind of music they played. He got through the gigs and he was paid well. In the high spirits at these events, the band often attracted very big tips, which Rafi's bandleader distributed more or less evenly. Tibor was soon earning more money than he could spend. He bought a new drum kit and drumming became his profession. He put most of his earnings as piles of cash on the kitchen table for his mum, not knowing what else to do with it. What else could he want, he had music and money and he was 17.

All the various bands' favourite hang-out in Haifa was The Moulin Rouge Café. It was a popular spot. It opened out onto an extremely wide pavement with tables and chairs under parasols. It had elegance and charm and was the haunt of local artists, particularly musicians, many of whom a couple of years earlier had been unreachable to Tibor. Now he was one of them. It felt like progress.

Chapter Six

The Army

All Israeli males serve three years in the military. Women serve for two years. A letter arrived in the mail for Tibor giving him a starting date for his military service and the location of the base where he had to report. When that date arrived he said goodbye to his family and friends and boarded an army bus. He was full of fear and trepidation, not knowing what to expect or what lay in store for him. After all his life could be put in danger and he could be injured in the course of doing this unavoidable duty. It was the law and he had no choice whatsoever in the matter. He had to go.

His drumming had to stop of course and the band was put on hold. As it happened Shimon the guitarist had received his call-up papers too but had avoided conscription by pleading insanity. He convinced the army psychiatrists that he was unstable and was therefore unsuitable material for the army. He played the game well and he was not the only one to pull off this stunt. Later it transpired that Shimon in fact sadly really did have a mental health problem.

Tibor's first day in the Israeli Army

The military transport bus headed deep into the countryside to the main Army Reception Base. First Tibor was sent to the barber's and his hair was cut short. He was then instructed to go to another room. As he passed through the doorway he was injected from the right and the left by a pressurized injection device by a medical person each side. Tibor felt like a sheep heading for slaughter. It was all highly organized and efficient. He completed the paperwork and was given a uniform and a huge kit bag. It was a soulless process and very unnerving. For the next few days the conscripts slept in ten-men tents, while they went through the induction process and the army decided where they thought they would be most effectively put to use and to which division they would be attached. Tibor went into his final interview with no idea where he'd be assigned or what his tasks could be. He crossed his fingers and hoped for the best.

The interviewer announced to Tibor that he had been assigned to the Military Police! It was explained to him that because he was an only child and his mother was a widow he would not be attached to a combat unit where his life would be put directly at risk. Although Tibor had no idea what his duties would be in the military police he was relieved and a spring came into his step as he left the interview.

A few days later he was sent to a camp where he started his Basic Training Course. Regardless of what unit you were attached to in the Israeli army the initial training was the same. He was taught how to handle weapons and went through the rigorous physical training course. It was hard graft with an early wake up and a run before breakfast and then the torture began again without a break, day in and day out. Fitness was not something that had much appeal to Tibor then and the course was demanding. The conscripts were pushed to the limits of their endurance. It was unpleasant but he knew that it wouldn't last forever.

Moroccan and Lebanese hashish was readily available in Israel and it was cheap. Often he had to do guard duty in the middle of the night. Guards were positioned in trenches or up on observation towers. There really was no security threat on this particular training base and some of the soldiers fell asleep. Tibor and some of his unit smoked joints to help pass the time. He had recklessly smuggled in some dope when he started military service and he would top up with some more when he could.

The training went on for three months. There were no females in his division and the men were pushed hard. The conscripts were occasionally allowed to go home for the weekend. Buses were laid on to Tel Aviv and from there, they mostly hitchhiked home. This was commonplace for soldiers in Israel and it still is. Getting a lift was never difficult as the general public were very supportive of their soldiers. There were specified hitching points along the roads, which were similar to bus stops.

The demanding training and the nightly guard duties tended to turn the young soldiers into zombies. Every day more was demanded of them.

Looking back Tibor has some particular memories one of which was grenade training. They were positioned in groups of three with an instructor behind an earth bank. They were shown how to pull the pin out of the grenades and they took it in turns to throw them. He didn't expect the handle to separate from the grenade in mid-air and right over his head with such a loud click. He had a moment or two of sheer terror but the grenade flew away from him and hit the ground with a huge explosion. They were also trained in the use of all the weapons in service in the army. They went through them all in great detail and were shown how to take them apart, clean them and put them back together again. Tibor was more interested in this side of the training. Understanding the working of the mechanisms suited the engineer in his character. They were then taken out onto a range and fired Kalashnikov AK47s, Belgian FN rifles and 9mm Uzis. One thing that struck Tibor was that he would not want to be hit by a round from an AK47. The bullets were very large and would clearly do a lot of damage to a body struck by a round from this weapon. Looking back he is glad that he had this experience and access to these weapons. Soldiers were all issued with the FN rifle and they were instructed to take it with them wherever they went and to have them at all times. It was a cumbersome weapon - long and heavy - and it wasn't even semi-automatic. They used this rifle on inspections and parades. His FN, Tibor recalls, was so clean that he could have performed brain surgery with it! He even had to take his meals with the rifle. It was certainly not a weapon though he would have chosen to go into battle with.

The three month training period finished and he was finally told where he was going to be posted. He would be guarding a jail at a place called Megiddo, which is to the south east of Haifa. The jail housed captured Arab soldiers and terrorists. This was for real and not a game. The prison was large and held hundreds of inmates. The cells were big and held something like 80 prisoners each. They slept in three tier bunks. Each cell opened onto an inner yard where the prisoners could cook. The guards supplied them with food and the prisoners prepared it for themselves. They were locked in their cells at night. Outside each cell door was a space like a porch where the guards sat. There was never any interaction between the guards and the prisoners even though they could see each other clearly. The guards were not armed but they carried tear gas canisters in case there was any trouble.

One night Tibor was on guard duty. It was very quiet and he could not stay awake so he sat down on the floor and promptly fell asleep. He woke in time for the change-over and thought that all was well. However, next day he was called to the prison Commanding Officer's office. Tibor sensed that something was up and that he was not going to be promoted to General that day! The CO was highly decorated and an impressive, fearsome figure. He told Tibor to sit and asked how the shift went last night. He responded that it had gone OK. The CO asked if he had fallen asleep and Tibor replied that he hadn't. The officer announced that he had evidence to the contrary and Tibor wondered how that could be. The CO explained that they had microphones hidden in the walls of the cells and the conversations between the prisoners were recorded. These recordings were listened to on a daily basis. The CO explained that they heard the prisoners discussing the fact that Tibor was asleep and they were coming up with ideas for killing him. One of them suggested that they could do this by stabbing him in the head with a long stick. Tibor was puzzled. He assumed the prisoners were aware that he didn't have keys, but they still talked about attempting to kill him, which was very strange. In the event the CO stopped his leave for 28 days, which was a tough punishment for Tibor as he relied on being able to get off the base and go home frequently.

In the following months a day came when the guards were instructed to assemble and they were briefed that all the prisoners were to be released en masse in exchange for the release of just a very few Israelis. This was common practice with perhaps as many as 500 Arab prisoners being exchanged for the release of as few as just one or two Israelis. The prison was emptied so a transfer became necessary for Tibor.

Chapter Seven
Prison Six

Prison Six just outside Haifa

Shortly after this Tibor was allocated to another prison, which was a bit closer to his home and just outside Haifa. It was called Prison Six and it was well known. It was there purely for the imprisonment of Israeli soldiers. Inmates were held there for up to 70 days maximum.

It was a very different prison from the previous one. The inmates were less of a security risk to the country. During the day the prisoners worked in the prison or were taken out to different bases to do work for the army. It was a slightly looser regime than before. There were no murderers amongst them, who would have liked to kill their guards. Their crimes were minor like going AWOL or some other moderate transgression.

Given the time spent in the army so far Tibor was promoted from private to corporal and was in line to be a Sergeant in the future. This pleased him as less and less soldiers would then be above him to tell him what to do.

There were several hundred prisoners in Jail Six. After breakfast they went on parade to have their appearance inspected. Tibor had to ensure that they had shaved and were looking presentable. They were then marched for a short time in the courtyard, until it was time to go to work. It was not a tough regime but was all part of the program to ensure that the prisoners would not want to transgress again and end up in prison. At 9:00pm they were locked in their cells, which were large and almost like those at Megiddo. The guards were able to relax. This was when they got stoned on hashish and beer from the canteen. Two guards remained on duty in an office overlooking the main yard, which gave access to the cells. The rest of the unit did as they pleased.

Tibor recalls that this was where he really learnt to smoke dope! He had one particular friend, whose background was Iranian. This friend showed him the technique of smoking dope through a potato. They would take a potato, carve out the inside, fill it with a mixture of tobacco and hash and stick a cardboard tube underneath. This was then placed in a tall half full glass of water. Then they put the tube between their fingers and, leaving just enough room, covered the top of the glass. When they took a hit the air entered the tube on the top of the potato and passed through the water, filtering the smoke like a water pipe. It really hit hard and they ended up very stoned indeed. The activity became a known fact amongst the prison guards. One weekend, when normally the officers were at home with their families, as usual they smoked dope through the potato pipe. Tibor's friend foolishly announced in a hushed voice over the Tannoy PA system for the whole jail to hear that; 'Tibor is smoking hashish'. Tibor wasn't upset or worried about this, as he realized it would be taken as a joke by everyone. However it stuck and for days afterwards he was teased about this by the others. It was meant to be a joke but there could have been trouble. In the event they were never caught, grassed on, or challenged by any of the officers. Had they been pulled up for it they could have ended up among the prisoners themselves.

There were some curious types of prisoners in the jail too. One interesting example was the Jehovah's Witnesses. Like every other young Israeli they had to serve in the military and do their three years, but their ideals caused them to resist. They simply refused to serve and were sent to jail for 70 days! On their release day they were asked if they would serve and again predictably, they refused and were put back in jail on the same day. On the whole Tibor liked them and found them to be intelligent and a good bunch of guys, who were very capable. So much so, that they willingly assisted in the management of the complex administration of the prison office. Tibor could see the irony of this because they were effectively upholding the system and in a way serving the military. If a job was left unfinished on their release date, due to their continued refusal to serve, the guards knew they would be sent back by the same evening to finish the job!

At the far end of the jail there were a few cells which opened into a yard and the doors were never locked. This was where Israeli fighter jet pilots were held and it was much more comfortable. They were the elite and they were well looked after by the regime. Tibor caught himself often glancing at them. He was in awe of them. His enthusiasm about flying had never left him. However much he wanted to interact and get to know them, it wasn't possible, due to time constraints. Even though he was a corporal in charge, he still felt far beneath these pilots. He respected these men.

Every day new prisoners came to the prison for their allotted 35 or 70 day sentence and every day some prisoners finished their sentence and were released. There was a high turnover. One evening Tibor was supervising supper. The prisoners stood in line, each picked up a stainless steel meal tray and metal cutlery then took their turn to have their food dished out and sat down to eat. That particular evening, one cocky, freshly arrived prisoner was not keeping in line, attempting to push ahead of the rest. Tibor decided to be firm with him and confronted the man. He was completely taken by surprise when the prisoner turned on him and came at him with a fork, stabbing him in the neck and nose. Blood poured from his wounds while the man was overpowered by other guards. Tibor was in shock and felt no immediate pain. It turned out that the wound in his neck was very close to a main artery and could have been life threatening. To this day he still carries small scars from the event. He was rushed to surgery where he was patched up, then sent home for a few days. Before he left, his boss came to see him. The officer was very athletic and reminded Tibor of Bruce Lee with his slightly oriental appearance. He explained to Tibor that the prisoner was safely locked up in solitary confinement in a separate division. They had beaten him. They took Tibor to see him and he was shocked. The prisoner looked in a quite a bad way. It was not something he would consider doing himself, but took some vengeful satisfaction after what had been done to him.

One of the Haifa bands had a really skilled drummer David Almishali, who Tibor admired enormously.

David Almishali

He was a god-like figure to Tibor. He looked majestic and elegant when drumming with his band, very thin with long dark straight hair and a pair of thick black rimmed glasses, reflecting the lights as if he was sending out sparks. He had plenty of style and he was certainly not suitable material for the army.

David turned up one day in Prison Six. He was brought in for desertion. At first Tibor couldn't believe his eyes, but it was indeed David the drummer. Immediately Tibor thought that here was a chance for him to help and take care of this special man. He took David out of the cells as much as he could and tried to prevent him even going near one, on days when he was in charge.

Tibor's shifts were two days on and two days off. He had plenty of spare time with this schedule, so he could think very seriously of playing again. He got things going and soon the band was rehearsing and taking bookings. They were back in business!

Tibor was occasionally recognised by people, who had been in Jail 6 under his jurisdiction and there were a few that wanted to take revenge on him. At one particular gig in Beit Shean after the van had just left the venue there was a large commotion on the road in front of them. They were forced to stop and the crowd demanded that Tibor get out and 'face the music'. In preparation for occasions like this he carried a canister of tear gas, which he intended to deploy in any attacker's face. It had almost come to this when suddenly and out of the blue one of the officers, Lt. Damari, from Jail 6 appeared by the van. He was a local guy and picked up on the trouble vibe. He told the crowd to disperse and to leave Tibor alone and, because Damari was well known to the locals, trouble was averted. He may well have saved Tibor's life.

The following week Tibor took an Uzi sub-machine gun from the weapon's store in case his life came under threat again. He kept it concealed in a shoulder bag at his feet next to the drums, hoping to God that he wouldn't need to use it!

At the end of another gig as they were packing up the gear (no roadies unfortunately) a couple of those lads came up to them and said, 'Forget about last week. We're sorry. Come and have a joint with us'. And they did. They smoked the pipe of peace and laid down their weapons!

At a certain point Beber, the singer, stormed out of the band. He had an inflammable personality like all singers! The others just said, 'OK. Let's find another singer.' They ended up with a girl called Sherry. She was the sister of a bass player from another Haifa band and she had an incredible rocky voice. With this new line-up the band became 'Silverspoon' - taken from the name of a song by an American band called Ursa Major - really heavy but punchy number. Real electricity!

After Tibor left Israel he was amazed to learn just how many of his contemporaries had made it and become super-famous and successful in that country. Sherry became a star and released a few albums, which she still performs live. Had he stayed, he would have had a job for life, playing with all his mates. It seems he was destined for even greater heights - right up to 37000 feet!

Word got about even penetrating through to the officers in the jail. They learnt that he was a drummer in a fairly successful band. This was during his third year in the military. He was often allowed extra hours out, if he had to play at an important gig. The officers were relaxed about this. Around the middle of that year Tibor was called up to see his Commanding Officer, who showed him a letter inviting him to join one of the Army Bands. The level of musicianship in these bands was very high and they played all over Israel even in the remotest areas. They also appeared on radio and television and were extremely popular with the general public too. They brought a lot of pleasure to the troops and were experts in their craft. There was a request for him to audition and it was explained that if he was accepted and joined a band he would have to spend an extra two to three years in the army. Tibor turned the offer down immediately and without a second thought. There was no way he was going to spend more time in the army. He had other plans and they were beginning to take shape.

Chapter Eight

Ktziot

During 1976 he was posted to the Negev Desert in the south of the country. This small base had recently been set up by the army at Ktziot, within which they had made provision for a number of prisoners from Jail Six to be accommodated in tents as an outpost for the main jail. These prisoners were used by the army during the day to work at other bases, amongst other things, packing and transporting munitions.

To start with a friend of his was tasked with running the prison section. He had made a good job of this, but he was due for rotation to another posting and they asked Tibor to take over. By this time he had been promoted to Sergeant and obviously had the required experience and expertise to handle the job.

Ktziot was in the desert and was far away from any towns or villages. There were other army bases around but nothing close. The base was isolated. The journey from Jail Six took around four hours. The last town on the way down was Beersheba, which was some 30 miles away.

After Beersheba the scenery completely changed to endless sand dunes stretching away into the distance with occasional scattered palms under a burning sun. On the drive they would pass Bedouins walking or riding their camels, leading goats across the wide expanses. The Bedouin were predominantly an Arab desert dwelling ethnic group, divided into clans or tribes. Tibor was impressed by their resilience particularly by how they survived with apparent ease in the desert heat. He watched them fascinated. He made occasional visits back to Jail Six by army transport to deliver prisoners and to escort other inmates awaiting release. He enjoyed those journeys through the desert.

Tibor relished the remoteness of the jail at Ktziot. He was attracted by the atmosphere of the place. The base reminded him of scenes from Wild West films with its small wooden buildings, canteen and kitchen/diner. Prisoners and guards lived in half a dozen big 10-bed tents. The sides could be rolled up so there was usually a good breeze running through them.

Life at the jail was easy going and very pleasant. It suited Tibor well and he thought it was a really great place to spend his remaining time in the army. He managed the jail while the reservists under his command did the work. The reservists were soldiers who had completed their three year conscription and were now obliged to serve in the army for 35 days each year until the age of 55.

Once a week Tibor supervised the arrival of new prisoners. It was an opportunity to catch up with friends at Jail Six, who escorted the inmates. Tibor welcomed the newbies with a speech, which introduced them to the rules and routines of the prison. He made the point that there were no fences around the base and that they were free to flee. No one had in fact ever deserted from there, as there was really nowhere to go. It was a bold and challenging thing to say but it worked. He stressed that the atmosphere was relaxed and that there was no better place to serve out a 35 or 70 day sentence. In fact the prisoners had been transferred to Ktziot because they had behaved well at Jail Six. All they had to do was carry on in the same way and the time would pass quickly and easily.

Tibor was King in the jail. He would stay in bed until nine by which time the prison was already empty. He had one prisoner retained to help him with his paperwork but otherwise the prison portion of the base was deserted throughout the day. While he was washing, his assistant would go to the kitchen and bring him his hot breakfast, which he plated and served to him in the tent. This was the highlight of his day and he loved it. The routine had been set up by his predecessor but Tibor was more than happy to keep it going. His team was successful in maintaining green plants around the tents that his predecessor had established. It gave the place a holiday camp atmosphere! Tibor was always careful to make sure the base brought the water bowser around at times just for watering the plants. Apart from watching out for Scorpions they also had to deal with frequent sand storms. Even with their tents buttoned down and secured, when it came, everything filled with sand or was coated with dust.

While the prisoners were left to relax in their own area, Tibor usually took his dinner with the reservists as a team, in the canteen. Then they had a couple of beers and occasionally some Vodka. Israel did not have an alcohol-orientated culture in those days. Tibor was just 22 and was not used to heavy drinking but there were times, when the drinking got heavy. He learnt where his limits lay the hard way.

He wasn't able to get home as much as he had been used to. He talked to his mother frequently by phone. On his journeys home after a few weeks in the desert he remembers being forcefully struck in Beersheba, by the of vivid colours of the buildings, gardens and the bright clothing people were wearing. Because all he had seen for weeks was desert, sand and the olive green of the tents and uniforms, his awareness and sensitivity to the use of colour in normal life was strongly aroused.

Overall, he was happy where he was and hoped to stay there until his army service was finished. However out of the blue he took a phone call from the senior officer at Jail Six who told him that unfortunately he had been posted to Ktziot in error. They had only just noticed that they had overlooked that he was a single child of a single parent and consequently as regulations had it, he should never have been put in a position that could be dangerous or at such a distance from his home, as this base was. This came as a blow to Tibor. Things were going very well and the living was easy but it had to change.

While he was at Prison Six, he became friends with another guard, Paul Greenstein. Paul was from England and represented everything English that intrigued Tibor. He and his parents lived on a Kibbutz. Tibor remembers that he read books in English avidly and recalls that Paul was reading *The Dice Man* by Luke Reinhard, at that time. He had the impression that the English were more cultured and musical than Israelis. Once or twice he visited Paul on the kibbutz where he met other guys from England, Canada and the US, who were his housemates. The group smoked and got stoned together. They spoke English but Tibor couldn't understand them all that well, which was frustrating. He resolved that he would learn English properly, just as soon as possible. Tibor had the overwhelming feeling that this was where he wanted to be, these were the kind of people he wanted to be among. He liked the flavour of their company and they liked him.

Eventually Tibor's three years of military service came to an end. He was transported to the collection base that he had arrived at three years ago. Last time he was there he had no idea what was going to happen to him. This time it was different. He signed out, handed over his kit bag with all his military gear and he was free. It was just like being released from prison! It was a really, really good day. Whoosh!

Chapter Nine

Back Behind a Drum Kit

Soon after he was released in early 1977 Tibor secured a choice contract to play in an open air nightclub in Nahariya, near the coast, just outside Haifa. He played every night with the resident band and the money was good. The band was backing an American black trio of singers. Two girls and a big, big bloke. He played there for two months. Tibor felt he had finally made it professionally. One night a fight broke out at the club over a go-go dancer. A customer claimed he had given the girl a big tip, which he assumed had bought her for the night. When the girl explained that this was not the deal the customer lost his temper, punches were thrown and chairs started to fly. It was a dirty fight and it spilled right out onto the street. This was too much for Tibor. There had been other ugly scenes before. It was a hot country and tempers flared easily. There were primarily two types of citizens in Israel. Those that came mainly from Marocco and other Arab backgrounds (Sfaradim) and those that had immigrated from more northern climes, or Europe,

(Ashkenazim). In Tibor's experience the fights were usually started by the Sfaradim. He made up his mind that night to get out of Israel as fast he could. He was determined to leave and he announced his decision to Róza. He was only 23, but he was bold and ready to try it. He had no firm plan of course, but he had the bravado of youth on his side. His mother conceded to his wish and supported him. She didn't argue with him but part of Tibor felt that he was letting her down. The drive to leave was strong in him and carried him along and he realized that he couldn't live his life for his mother. He had to make his own decisions, blaze his own trail and follow his desire.

The night before he left for the UK he and his mum stayed with his Uncle Alex, whose flat was conveniently near the airport. That evening he went into Tel Aviv with his cousin Miki to the cinema. They watched David Bowie in *The Man Who Fell to Earth*. It was the perfect film to watch on his last night in Israel and leaving his old life behind. The following day Alex and Róza dropped him at the airport and he boarded his flight. This time the aircraft was an impressive Boeing 747. He found himself sitting next to a girl, who introduced herself as Rivki. They fell into conversation and Tibor told her he was a drummer. It turned out that she was the ex-girlfriend of the most famous drummer in Israel. His name was Ariel Kaminski and he was very good. Tibor was taken aback by this coincidence. Rivki explained that she now had a boyfriend in England and they were moving in together. They had a house in North London, which they were renovating. While the work was going on, she and her boyfriend were living in a flat. Rivki offered him a place to stay if he had nowhere else to go and if he would contribute some of his time to working on the house renovations. Before they parted company she gave him her phone number in case he wanted to follow up on the offer. Tibor had another Israeli friend from Haifa, who was currently in the UK called Yossi Cohen. It was reassuring that he did have at least one contact in the UK. They had agreed that Tibor would get in touch with him once he had arrived. Yossi was staying with relatives in Preston and he had explained to Tibor that he could get a coach at Victoria Station and then travel north. Tibor accepted the offer and Yossi met him at the bus terminal, then took him back to the house where he was staying. He didn't of course plan on staying there long because London was where he wanted to be - at the heart of things. Whilst settling in, one of the first things that struck him was the milk-man and his morning deliveries. He'd never experienced anything like this before.

After a week or so he contacted Rivki and she said that the offer was still open so he and Yossi travelled down to London. The house had largely been gutted. There were no carpets, but there was running water and electricity. It was October and it was starting to get cold. They worked on the house, but were short of cash so Tibor needed to find a paying job.

As a tourist it was illegal to take paid work, but Tibor heard of an agency in Hammersmith which could find jobs for people in their position without work permits. They would turn up in the morning to be driven in a minibus to a factory or some such, where they were looking to hire cheap labour. The work was hard and dirty. On one occasion they ended up in the Hoover Building on the A40, moving furniture to clear a room. Tibor was very impressed by the building.

On another day they were taken to a perfume factory where he met a South African called Selwyn and his girlfriend Helen. Selwyn was a talented musician - a multi-instrumentalist, who wrote, played bass, keyboards and guitar. Tibor told Selwyn that he was also a musician, a drummer, and they struck up an immediate friendship.

Soon, following this meeting, Tibor contacted Róza and asked if she and Beber could pack up his drum kit and arrange to have it transported to the UK. They agreed to do this and Beber to his credit went to a lot of trouble putting one drum shell inside another, packing all the skins and cymbals on top. All the stands were folded up and the kit was packed into a remarkably small cardboard box. Eventually Tibor received a message telling him that he had some cargo to pick up from Heathrow, which he collected, took back to his place and assembled.

After two or three months Yossi moved on to live in America. Selwyn and Helen were living in West Hampstead. Tibor rented a tiny, one room apartment in the same area. There was a sink in the room, but no toilet. This was located on the floor below. But he was self-sufficient, going to work every day, paying his rent and trying to get a foot on the bottom rung of the musicians' ladder.

His six month visa was about to expire. He had to do something about this and quickly. Earlier on he had made friends with a guitarist called Roland who told him that the best way to stay in the UK on a permanent basis was to get married. He told Tibor that for a small amount of money changing hands he knew a girl called Viv who would go through with this marriage of convenience. She was living with a man and they had three children. They were divorced but strangely continued to live together in harmony. They had split before and then got back together again. Viv agreed to the marriage for just £100! Tibor heard that some rich Arabs had been known to marry in the UK and pay as much as £10,000. So this was a very good deal and Tibor knew it. They booked a slot at Marylebone Registry Office and Viv turned up with two friends, who were prepared to serve as witnesses. She had a ring and she was surprisingly well dressed. They went through the ceremony. He put the ring on her finger, gave her a kiss and that was that. What followed was not so simple though. He had popped up on the Home Office's radar and now he had to make the marriage look authentic to the authorities. In fact, he had never had a proper relationship with Viv. They had only talked to make their story more plausible.

Tibor left the agency and started to look for other work. He heard that there was a vegetarian restaurant called Pippin up in Hampstead, run by an Israeli. He hoped that the proprietor Joe would give him a job. He walked up to Hampstead, found the restaurant and went in. Vegetarianism was catching on in the UK and the huge restaurant was rammed. It had an impressive flagstone floor with many huge wooden tables and benches. The excellent food was cooked on site and there was a wide selection on the menu. It was very attractive and beautifully decorated, opening out onto Hampstead High Street. It looked and felt good and he immediately wanted to work there. He went up to the counter and asked for Joe. He waited and when Joe appeared Tibor asked him if he had any work. Joe asked him what he could do and Tibor responded that he could do whatever was required of him. Joe said that they needed help with cleaning and washing up, which he knew he could handle. He got the job. It was hard work. He started at 8am and often worked as late as 10pm. The days were long and he spent them carrying deliveries from the street down into the basement. He washed up and cleared tables. Tibor discovered that the restaurant was owned by the Peake family, which had a big holding in the highly successful Copella apple juice business.

Tibor's attention was caught early on by a girl working at Pippin. She had blonde hair and wore striking red clogs every day. She worked part time, arriving in the morning, leaving again in the early afternoon. She worked behind the counter on the ground floor. Her name was Libby and they struck up a friendship right away and connected. Even though his English was still far from perfect, they talked a lot and he found out that she had a son called Bill, who was six at the time. She explained that she had broken up with Bill's father, Storm Thorgerson, the mastermind behind Hipgnosis, the world's most well known record sleeve design company. Libby asked if he had heard of Hipgnosis and Tibor said that he had. One day back in Israel when he was very stoned, sitting on a carpet somewhere listening to Pink Floyd he became immersed in its cover and while studying it all over, he had noticed the words 'Sleeve design by Hipgnosis'. No one there could explain to him what that meant. He could tell it had nothing to do with hypnosis as such so it made no sense to him. He had never forgotten this though and it totally blew his mind that he had finally met someone linked to that puzzle. Here he was struggling to get started with his musical career only to meet up with someone well connected to no less than Pink Floyd!

During this time Tibor was still in touch with Selwyn and they worked together on his music. He was always checking out the advertisements at the back of Melody Maker magazine where there were classified ads for jobs in bands. He studied these on a regular basis. As a result he managed to join up with a band based in Maida Vale, which he thought had some potential. He also followed up on another ad for a drummer.

These people asked him to come up to a flat in Uxbridge without his drums to audition. He climbed up the tower block, found the number and pressed the doorbell. The door was opened by a woman and he was led into a very domestic scene. There were two children in the bath. She asked Tibor to go through to the lounge, which was simply furnished with a couple of bean bags and a sound system. Three or four fairly mature, serious looking guys, slightly older than Tibor, were waiting for him. They asked who he was and checked him off against their list and after a short conversation, then proposed that he listen to some of their music to see what he thought of it. They offered him a joint, sat him down and he listened to several tracks, which he slowly realized, were not really in line with his musical taste. It was very middle-of-the-road compared to his kind of heavier rock, but he recognised immediately that they were extremely talented. After another short discussion, they told him that they would let him know if they wanted to take things further. He never heard from them again and then years later he was watching a music show on TV and gradually realized that who he was watching seemed very familiar. Suddenly it came to him, they were Dire Straits! Even now their music is not his kind of thing and he finds the drumming boring and very mainstream. Of course they're multi-millionaires now and he would certainly have taken the job for the money! They must have thought from the conversation that he might not fit their style, even though they have never heard him play and they let him go. It was however a good example of what following up a little ad in Melody Maker can lead to.

He carried on rehearsing with the Maida Vale band at a four storey squat in Formosa Street. The place was run by a guitarist called Bob. He was the boss there and he virtually 'owned' the place. There was a rehearsal room in the basement, which was carpeted on floors and ceiling as well as on the door. It was soundproof and when they played there, no one could hear them. Apart from Bob and Tibor they had a bassist, John, and another guitarist called Alan, but they realized that they badly needed a lead singer. They had all sorts of weird and wonderful people coming to them to audition. On one occasion a more mature guy turned up, who went by the name of Elmer Gantry. He was chosen by the band for looking the part, with his exceptionally raunchy and professional sounding voice and they decided to call themselves 'Gantry'. Elmer took his name from the part played by Burt Lancaster in the film of the same name. He was relatively well known in the business. He sang in the stage version of Hair and he had a band called Stretch. The band had a hit in the 60s with a track called *Why Did You Do It?*

One afternoon another of Elmer's endless connections in the business came to the basement rehearsal studio with him. He didn't bother to introduce him to the rest, as he was running late that day. This man, in a peaked cap stood by the door and didn't say anything, all afternoon. He just listened to them playing. At the end of the session he left with Elmer again without speaking. This was typical of Elmer. When he returned the next week for a rehearsal he gave Tibor a used Premier bass drum pedal, which was not something he expected a singer to be carrying. Tibor looked puzzled and Elmer explained. He reminded Tibor about last week's visitor and told him the mystery man had been very impressed by his drumming and wanted Tibor to accept the pedal as a present and told him that it was Ian Pace the drummer with Deep Purple. Wowww! Now Pace was one of Tibor's great heroes, who he really admired. He would have fainted, had he known who it was at the time! Pace was an extraordinarily gifted drummer and absolutely impossible to imitate.

Elmer Gantry (aka Dave Terry) had many other connections in the music business. At one point he arranged for them to exchange their carpet-clad, airtight, no-outside-light rehearsal room to one much nicer located on a farm in Wisley, near Woking. This farm and the building were owned by **The Moody Blues**! The band members were not living there, but the drum roadie John was. He was looking after the place and they were given use of the facilities for free! Amazing stuff. One day at lunchtime they were rehearsing when suddenly this guy walked in with a big 70s type moustache, seemingly having had a few drinks too many. He said a few incomprehensible words then staggered out. Minutes later he was back with a flute in his hand. They started jamming to a bluesy-type mood in which he seemed to find solace! He was **Ray Thomas** of **The Moody Blues**. It was fun. He was a warm and gentle guy.

Tibor continued to work at Pippin and one day Storm Thorgerson came in to see Libby to drop something off for her. She introduced him to Storm. Tibor had already met Bill their son on a couple of occasions when she picked the boy up from school. He understood that Bill lived with his father. When he knew Storm a little better he explained that he was a drummer in a band that was starting to sound good and that they were looking for a manager. Storm confirmed that he knew John Sherry, the manager of 'Wishbone Ash' and that he might be the right kind of guy to take on 'Gantry'. He arranged for Sherry to come to the studio with his partner Rod Linton to sit in on a rehearsal and to listen to them play through a set. They turned up, listened and decided that the band were good enough to go for a recording session. Sherry booked them into De Lane Lea studios in Wembley to cut a demo tape. The band was delighted and Tibor was over the moon. He had seen the name De Lane Lea mentioned on several album covers from the past and knew it was a serious place to record. Through Elmer, Tibor managed to set himself up with a new and much classier Tama drum kit for the event and for the future.

They went into De Lane Lea for two days to record two tracks, completed the mastering and they finished the job on time. Sherry paid for the sessions and promised to do his best to get them a record deal, but in the event inexplicably he did nothing with the master tapes and puzzlingly, they never heard from him personally again. (Welcome to the music business!). At that time Tibor and the band were shocked and very disappointed. Linton kept promising that they would pull something off, but they never did any more for them. It was a big let-down. It started to dawn on Tibor that the music business is very tough and can be ugly. He was beginning to be disillusioned by it all.

Libby told him that she had a boyfriend called Sam, who lived in West Hampstead and that he had a spare room in his flat, which Tibor could possibly take for a very reasonable rent. Tibor couldn't wait to escape from his dingy, one room accommodation in the same district and jumped at the chance to move. He looked at the room. It was in a really nice flat, with access to gardens in a good location for work and he took up the offer. Unfortunately, some months later Sam explained that Libby was going to move in with him and that he would need Tibor's room in the near future. As a result of this, with Bob's agreement Tibor has decided to move in with the band at Formosa Street, into the squat.

Life in the squat was OK with people continuously coming and going there was not much privacy, but plenty of things happening - lots of rehearsals and never boring.

Since he wasn't regularly drinking a lot of alcohol he only occasionally went down to the local pub with Bob, John and the rest. Bob in particular liked to drink heavily. One evening Tibor decided to stay in the flat. Bob had a rescued cat which was quite mutilated. It was badly scratched and it had no whiskers on one side of its head and only one ear. It was a very warm and friendly animal, even though it had obviously been very badly treated by someone in the past. The cat had become pregnant and was starting to look enormous. Tibor was sitting alone in the lounge when he noticed in amazement, that the cat was starting to give birth. He thought that nature would take care of itself, so he sat and watched while it gave birth to the first kitten. It lay still in its amniotic sack and the mother just walked away to another corner of the room. Tibor was puzzled and didn't know what to do for the best. He watched but the kitten wasn't moving. It looked dead. He thought he *needed* to do something. So he took a pair of scissors and cut open the sack and after waiting a few minutes, he also cut the umbilical cord linking the kitten to the placenta. He cut at what he thought was a good spot. Once it was cut the kitten let out a tiny sound, but the mother heard it, raced over and started to lick it. At which point another kitten popped out followed by another. Tibor carefully unpeeled each of the sacks surrounding these kittens too. By the time the last one arrived, there was a loud kitty-chorus going on, keeping the mother running from one to the other, increasingly confused. He bundled them all into a cardboard box, where they all settled. Bob, on his return from the pub, was extremely pleased to have missed the drama but to have ended up with some 7 kittens and a healthy mother. Tibor resolved to keep that first kitten and John suggested the name Benny and the name stuck. He lived with Tibor through thick and thin, becoming a brother to a dog and a human baby, for 16 happy years.

The journey from the squat to Pippin was considerable and he found himself a discarded bicycle. He continued to work but he was getting tired of the job.

He knew that at some point he would be receiving a sudden visit from the Home Office to verify that he and Viv were living together. He knew it was a mad notion but he thought it would be good idea to have a box of toys and some kids' clothes in his room, which he could scatter around at a moment's notice, if he ever had a visit, saying his wife was out with her 3 children. In any event he did not receive a visit at this time. He did have to report any change of address to the police as he was classed as an alien. An alien! Tibor still has the record book.

Chapter Ten

The Home Office

While Tibor was living in the squat in Maida Vale he and Viv were summoned by the Home Office to attend an interview at Lunar House in Croydon. He contacted Viv to let her know that they had been called in. They were to be interviewed on the same day but separately, so they had to get their stories straight. They met early at a café outside Lunar House and went over these things: where they met, their domestic arrangements even their nonexistent sex life. Tibor was very nervous. Lunar House was a most intimidating place. He was first to be called in, to an office with huge windows at the back. It had a Russian feel about it like something out of a spy thriller. There was one immaculately dressed interviewer, who was in fact quite pleasant. He asked Tibor a series of personal questions which he answered to the best of his ability. As he gave his answers he realized what a good thing it was that he and Viv had met beforehand to agree on their story. They had made more or less the correct assumptions about what they would be quizzed on. The interview lasted about 40 minutes and he was asked to go out and send in his wife. In the few seconds they had together, he went over some questions and his answers with Viv and she went in. Tibor was shaking. Eventually she came out with the interviewer and he said that they would be in touch again in due course and they were free to go.

Following the interview Tibor found himself feeling very paranoid at times from the threat of a sudden and unannounced visit. The meeting had been a success but just the same it was unsettling. Soon after, he received a letter from the Home Office telling him that he no longer had to report any change in his address, but there always remained the threat of an unexpected call hanging over him.

The Romance Blossoms

Libby and Tibor got on well at work and were starting to form an emotional attachment, but nevertheless, he decided to quit Pippin. He said his farewells and thought that was that. He didn't realize it then, but Libby didn't like him leaving, as it was no fun for her anymore and soon left the job herself. They kept in touch. Tibor signed on for unemployment benefit for a while, which gave him more time to work with the band. During the daytimes, he frequently cycled up to West Hampstead to visit Libby at Sam's flat. He was a mathematics student at University and was often out during the day. Tibor and Libby spent some happy times there together and their friendship strengthened rapidly. One day when they were setting out to collect Bill from school Libby turned to Tibor and asked, 'Do you think I love you?' He was taken aback and it nearly knocked him off his feet. Was she really in love with him he wondered. He didn't know how to respond, given that she had a relationship with Sam and there were Storm and Bill to take into account. This thing, he realized, could get very complicated. They went out and picked up Bill but Tibor was electrified. Eventually it happened and they went to bed together and after that everything changed.

Tibor's marriage was a small complication but Libby's relationship with Sam was a bigger problem. She had to make a decision and much to his amazement she chose Tibor! She told Sam and moved out, but she could not move back into her own flat as it was already being let out. She moved into the squat with Tibor but since he was sharing a room with Bob, she couldn't move in there. They put a mattress in the basement rehearsal room next to his drum kit. She brought some personal stuff over to the squat and they slept in the rehearsal room.

Libby had a silver Simca and they used it to move a few of her belongings over to the squat from Sam's. They were carrying some big Busy Lizzy plants from the car and were stopped by a policeman who accused them of carrying drugs. He was serious and they had to hold back their laughter. He thought it was Marijuana so they suggested to him that he take a leaf with him to have it checked by his drug squad. He let them go and when he was completely out of sight they cracked up. Hilarious!

After separating from Storm, Libby's parents helped her to buy a flat in Kentish Town. At the time she lived there she had a couple of tenants renting a bedroom each from her.

Now, Libby gave notice to quit to her tenants and they soon moved out from the flat in Leverton Street, Kentish town. This then allowed the couple to move into their own place but as they needed some additional income they let a spare room to John the bassist and his girlfriend Sue, who then left the squat and moved in.

The flat was on the top floor of the building and after the squat it was very civilized. It was on two levels with a kitchen, a bathroom, two bedrooms downstairs and a spiral staircase leading up to the top floor with one well lit, large attic room, with windows on two sides.

At this point neither of them worked, but they were eking out a living from a small regular income of Libby's from her family and Tibor's minimal benefits. At around this time, they have discovered whilst looking through some of Libby's documents that she had some money she was unaware of! It was a sufficient amount to make a significant difference to their lives and relieved any immediate financial pressure. They felt very lucky!

Tibor continued to work with the band. With John and Sue in residence, they had some good mornings, often with coffee and a joint for breakfast. Tibor still had the box of toys in case of a visit from the Home Office. He had let Viv have his new address.

Then there was an extraordinary and very fortunate coincidence. Another example of how good luck played a part in Tibor's story. One Saturday, they were having breakfast with John and Sue when the doorbell rang. It was Viv! She was asking to be let in. It was astonishing and unexpected, as she has never been to visit before but she said she was passing in the area and wanted to see where 'she was living' officially! She came upstairs, joined them in the kitchen for a coffee and they chatted amiably and were glad to see each other. Pretty soon after this, the doorbell rang again! Libby picked up the entry phone and announced that it was a POLICEMAN! He was asking to see Tibor and Viv! While he was making his way upstairs, they quickly threw the windows open to clear the lingering smell of Marijuana then let the lone policeman into the flat, ushering him carefully past the kitchen, straight upstairs to the attic room. He said he came on behalf of the Home Office and wanted to speak to Tibor first. Tibor offered him a drink and he asked for tea. He went downstairs to make the drink and told Viv not to leave under *any* circumstances. There and then, she took out her papers and changed her address, by hand, to 36 Leverton Street in case the policeman wanted to check them.

Tibor took the tea upstairs and even though he was very stoned he kept his composure and answered the questions that were put to him. It became clear to him that he was just a policeman from the local station and certainly not a professional representative of the Home Office. The interview with Tibor lasted fifteen minutes and then he was asked by the officer to send his wife up to see him. For a minute Tibor wondered which one! He had a quick word with Viv and then she went upstairs. Tibor waited in the kitchen full of fear and trepidation. He could not conceive that having got so far, it could all go wrong at this point. He needed his British residency to be made completely legal and secure.

As Tibor let the policeman out he asked what conclusions he had reached and he was told was that everything was fine and that the Home Office would be informed, so Tibor could expect a letter from them shortly. A confirmation of his British Citizenship arrived soon after and he was able to apply for a British passport, which was essential to him. Apart from anything else he very much wanted to visit Róza again in Israel. He had been back visiting his mother before but annoyingly, each and every time, there was a procedure to be gone through. He was obliged to report at the main Collecting Base where he had first been admitted into the army, in order to collect a clearance form, which had to be handed in at the border control upon his exit. Now, this irritating and time wasting formality would be a thing of the past. As a British citizen he could go to Israel and not be required to serve his annual reservist duty in the Israeli Army. He felt that the three years he had already given them in the military police was quite enough - more than enough!

With his British passport in his hand he went to the Israeli Embassy in London to revoke his citizenship. This went well and he received confirmation of the completion of this process in the post.

At the beginning of 1978 Libby's father became seriously ill. They had to go to Cambridge. Tibor had never visited her parents' home, or the city before. Libby drove them to Cambridge as Tibor didn't yet have a license. They arrived at the house, which was in Shelford on the outskirts of Cambridge. It was a huge property set in large grounds and with a private drive. She had never told him about this and it blew him away. Libby took Tibor in to meet her mother, who must have been shocked when she caught sight of him in his torn, paint-stained jeans and his long hair. He was also ten years younger than her daughter. As he remembers it was a very cold meeting. Tibor was not introduced to Libby's father, who remained in bed. Libby showed Tibor round the enormous house and the gardens. She pointed out the doorway where Hipgnosis had shot the cover for the Pink Floyd album *Ummagumma* with its infinite regressions. The design had been Libby's idea and

Tibor was very impressed. Tibor remembers the endless daffodils in the garden so he knows that they made that visit in the spring.

On the way back to London while Tibor was still recovering, Libby told him that the family also had a house at Blakeney in Norfolk close to the sea. She suggested that they go there and stay for a few days. Again Tibor was in for another shock. On the outside the house looked small but once they went in he knew the impression had been false. They entered onto the middle floor and he could see that the house was in fact laid out on three levels. It was a beautifully converted open plan barn with exposed beams. There were two bedrooms on the lower level and a lounge and kitchen on the ground floor with another bedroom on the top floor. They stayed there for a few days, returning in early January, which was when their son Jody was conceived calculating back from the time his birth on 6th October 1980. The 6th October is a highly significant date for Tibor as this was the date when he first arrived in the UK, three years earlier. They spent the Christmas of '79 in Blakeney and had a wonderful time there. They have continued to visit Blakeney over the years often going there as many as four times a year. Tibor fell in love with Norfolk then and continues to love going there. He found Norfolk to be totally different to anywhere else in England with its own rhythm and atmosphere. From their first visit he has always felt safe and comfortable there. Over the years they have considered moving to Norfolk but haven't done so yet.

One day around 1979 Libby and Tibor were at Heathrow flying off somewhere when she suddenly spotted David Gilmour standing on his own in the terminal. They stopped in front of him. He looked at them and exclaimed very warmly, 'Libby!' They embraced like old friends. She then introduced Tibor to David.

Some months later, they were invited to spend the day at David's home in Harlow where Tibor gave him a cassette of some songs he played on in the hope that David would not be able to resist getting involved with him musically, but he's still waiting! The day was very pleasant. They watched videos, which no one has ever seen, of Pink Floyd and he showed them 'all those guitars' in his studio including the world's first Fender Strat numbered 001.

There was no one else home that day. All the items of furniture and television had little labels on them with their names on, like 'table', 'telly' etc. At a guess it was for the benefit of the youngest child they had at that time and not for his guests.

Tibor met David on a number of occasions after this. Once at the sad funeral of their mutual friend Judy Trim, who was Roger Water's ex-wife. They spent a few minutes talking about Tibor's job as a Boeing 737 captain, which David related to very much. He told Tibor that he owned about 15 different aircraft himself!

They also met once at Abbey Road Studio II (OK, Tibor is now dropping names and locations too) where Storm had decided to organise the launch of one of his books that evening. It was in the very same room where the Floyd recorded Dark Side of the Moon in 1973! Tibor felt he was *ON* the moon listening to a speech by Storm mentioning this very fact, but looking at David with one eye at the same time!

Life went on in Leverton Street and Jody's birth was approaching. Bill was with them a lot - almost daily - mainly after they had picked him up from school. There were constant arrangements regarding his transport from their flat to Storm's and vice versa. Sometimes he came with a friend. Sometimes these friends' parents were 'utilised' by Storm to carry out the transporting.

Bill was about 10 when they moved from London to Farnborough, Hants. Jody was just one. The boys' relationship grew and they were always very good together and still are to this day.

Tibor still had his cat Benny. They had a litter tray under the spiral staircase but the only way it could go out was on the roof. The flat was in a terraced house and he could run along the roofs. He often went out for hours but one day he didn't come back. It was very unusual and despite Tibor searching the streets for days, there was no sign of him. Gradually after a few days, having given up hope, Tibor had the idea of getting a dog and he put this to Libby and she agreed. John and Tibor went to Battersea Dogs' Home. There were many dogs there but they were both very taken with a little black and white puppy, which looked at them pleadingly with its head cocked on one side. They picked him and took him home, with a little red collar provided by the Home. Although he was only a puppy he had a name, Toby, which had been given to him by his previous owner. On the first evening they took him for a walk around the block and when they got back to the front door of the house, to their utter surprise, amazement and disbelief, there was Benny, The Cat, just sitting there!

Incredibly, he had never been let out through this front door so it was all the more clever of him to find it and then sit and wait there. Looking at Benny they could see that one of his back legs was injured. They assumed he must have fallen off the roof. They took both Benny and Toby upstairs. Now, they had two animals to care for. Had they made a mistake? In any event they slowly became used to each other. Apart from Toby occasionally rooting around in the cat litter the family settled in together well. They had lovely, long daily walks up to Hampstead Heath with Toby. Libby was pregnant and Tibor was soon to be a father. Cat, dog and baby - it was amazing, everything was coming together and a family was forming.

Then another ship sailed onto Tibor's horizon. He was still friendly with Selwyn, who told him that he had a friend coming over from South Africa called Trevor Rabin, who had been in a band called Rabbitt, the top rock band in Capetown with Trevor being its main man. Selwyn and Trevor originally met in South Africa, playing in the same army band. Trevor was coming to the UK with his girlfriend Shelly and was going to crash on Selwyn's floor for a few days while he attempted to get a record deal as a solo artist in the UK.

Trevor had already made his first extraordinary solo album in South Africa which, when he heard it, totally blew Tibor away. It was very much his kind of music. Like Selwyn, he was a multi-instrumentalist and played everything except the drums. In South Africa he used a very good drummer called Kevin Kruger. When Tibor heard the album he thought he had stumbled across his destiny. More than anything he wanted to work with Trevor. They met in Selwyn's flat.

Trevor went up daily to central London and he had soon interested a management company in taking him on. They were helping to find a record company for him to sign with. Every day he came back with stories of the people he was meeting like Jeff Beck and Freddie Mercury. He was moving in the big time. Tibor was convinced that Trevor was going to make it huge and he wanted him to hear Gantry with a view to putting the band in touch with one of his many connections. He suggested this to Trevor who said he was interested to hear the band. He came to the rehearsal studio with Shelly. They all smoked a joint then played through a set. Trevor sat and listened. More than anything Tibor wanted Trevor to hear *him* drum. After they had played they went to the pub for a drink. There wasn't much discussion about the band at that time and soon after, Trevor announced that they had to go. Tibor suggested that he walk with them to their car and on the way he asked what he thought of the band. Trevor replied that the band was OK, but to his absolute amazement, he then said that he thought his drumming was excellent, so much so, that he wanted Tibor to become *his* drummer. Tibor felt his life was changing there and then and all in that very second! He said to Trevor that he couldn't believe what he was hearing and asked him to repeat it, turning to Shelley, saying 'you are my witness'! Trevor said it again and he felt his dream was starting to become a reality.

He knew he couldn't say anything to the band at this early stage but he could hardly wait to tell Libby. Trevor explained that he already had a contract in South Africa to make another solo album and that he was going to have Kevin Kruger play drums on it. All the tracks were already written he simply had to go there do the recording and would be away for three months after which he was set to return to the UK to put a band together and start touring. Before they left, Trevor and Shelly invited Tibor and Libby to visit them. They had rented a big bungalow in north London near Hendon. Trevor gave Tibor a pre-factory press vinyl copy of his previous album. He wrote down the track numbers and titles of the songs, on the blank label at the centre and suggested to Tibor that he study and learn them. Tibor loved the music. It was powerful yet still commercial with plenty of work for a drummer. Tibor was on cloud nine and took this special record as a sign of Trevor's commitment to him. It was truly a high point in his life. The highest ever as far as music goes.

Three months later Selwyn called him and asked, 'Guess who I was playing with today?' He then went on to say that he had been rehearsing with Trevor as a stand-in bass player. The penny dropped and Tibor realized that they had started rehearsals and without him as drummer! He telephoned Trevor and confronted him. Trevor apologized and said that he didn't know how to tell Tibor that his deal with Chrysalis stipulated that he join with a band formally called Bebop Deluxe with their own drummer and that he had no choice in the matter, if he wanted to have a record deal. That was that. Rehearsals had to start and Selwyn was the temporary bassist. They were going to go on tour, as a support act to a well known guitarist called Steve Hillage. Tibor's dream crumbled to dust right there and then. It was a terrible shock and a huge disappointment. But there was nothing at all he could do about it. He just had to accept it. He was very depressed.

Out of the blue tickets arrived to Selwyn's address for a gig at Hammersmith Odeon. Tibor went with Libby, Selwyn and Helen. They sat through Trevor's set and Tibor was delighted. Trevor's band sounded so bad and the reason for this was that he'd been grafted onto another band and the drummer didn't have a clue, or any feeling for the music. He knew that Trevor was a perfectionist. He grew up in a musical family. His father was the leader of major orchestra in Cape Town. This was embarrassingly below Trevor's highest of standards. The tour continued to its conclusion, but that was the end of Trevor's solo career. Later on he released a couple of other solo albums, featuring world class names, such as Jack Bruce, Manfred Mann, Simon Philips and others. Tibor did not speak to Trevor again.

He did hear that a while later Trevor had joined a new megaband which was called Asia and which sprang from the roots of some of the members of Yes, a band that always had a big turn-over of personnel and was the strongest influence on Tibor's musical taste, maybe even more than Led Zeppelin, Genesis and Deep Purple. He was a huge fan. They performed in stadiums to huge crowds. Yes was constantly forming and reforming around its core members. The drummer in Asia was Carl Palmer from Emerson, Lake and Palmer and Steve Howe was the lead guitarist who had been with Yes from inception. This struck Tibor as very odd because Trevor was also to be a lead guitarist. In the event he didn't stay in the band for very long. Much to Tibor's amazement Trevor Rabin moved over to join Yes filling the vacuum of Steve Howe and they released some albums together. One of the hits from those days was the single, written by Trevor, *Owner of a Lonely Heart*. He stayed with the band for 13 years and they continued to be hugely successful globally. The episode is still a painful memory for Tibor. This was his biggest near miss in the music world ever!

Chapter Eleven
Jody

In October 1980 Libby's waters broke. By this time Tibor had passed his driving test and at around midnight they made the inevitable dash to the hospital. On the way they stopped for Tibor to buy some cigarettes. He was going to be the traditional father, pacing up and down, smoking in the waiting room. In the early hours of the morning a nurse came out and told him that *it* was happening. There were no complications, except a dire need for oxygen for a short time. During the rush the nurse forgot to switch the oxygen bottles from the empty to the full one and Libby was near enough suffocated. Shortly after this rather alarming episode his baby son was born. Tibor remembers that he looked angry. He was frowning as if he resented being disturbed.

Unlike how things are in the UK today, in those early days they didn't know what sex the baby would be. A few days earlier Tibor and Libby had been strolling through Portobello Market when a complete stranger came up to them and announced that the baby she was carrying was a boy and he was right! After his son was born Tibor felt somehow vulnerable as if he had done his job of reproduction and that his life might be over but he was nonetheless overjoyed. Of course in reality he was no more vulnerable than he had been during Libby's pregnancy. He was very tired, went home and straight to bed for a few hours. They hadn't yet decided on a name for him.

In the early afternoon he returned to the hospital with a huge bunch of flowers for Libby. When he came out of the lift she happened to be in the corridor wearing a Chinese kimono style, bright red, full length robe and looking very slim! He had forgotten what she looked like before her pregnancy. He went in and picked up his little baby boy feeling very proud of himself. Later on Storm and Bill came to visit as did Libby's sisters Rosie and Susy with husbands and her mother Winnie and aunty Kath from Cambridge. After a couple of days she was allowed home and out of the blue Viv rang to ask about the baby. She asked if they had chosen a name yet and Tibor said they had a few ideas but hadn't decided. Viv suggested the name Jody. Tibor didn't know anyone by that name. Viv had the idea from the F1 racing driver Jody Scheckter. He put it to Libby and she liked it, so Jody it was. The girl he had married for just £100 had given them the name of their son! It was quite something.

When Jody was around two months old Storm rang. He asked if they could help him out with a baby! He explained that he was working on a project for 'The Police' who were about to release a new single called *De do do do De da da da*. This project required a few sinister looking men and a very gentle little baby and he thought Jody would just fit the bill.

Libby thought a nappy change may be in order, after which Tibor got into a cab with Jody in a baby basket and headed down to Denmark Street, known as 'Tin Pan Alley', in the centre of London. At the Hipgnosis studio Storm was very thankful and he said it wouldn't take long. While Jody was being photographed Tibor was wandering around the rooms. He could feel the enormous presence of the mega-bands that had graced this place in the past. Suddenly, tucked behind a load of discarded artwork, ideas in progress, dusty files and the remains of an old sandwich he noticed an object, the top of which was just peeking out.

Tibor at Hipgnosis with the Led Zeppelin 'object' by his right elbow

He thought he recognised it, but he couldn't believe his eyes. He pulled it out and *yes*, it was exactly what he thought it was. It was indeed the dark object used on one of Led Zeppelin's album covers *Presence*! It was fairly small, but its meaning was quite enormous in the world. In his younger days in Israel listening to this album, he often sat and gazed at the multitude of pictures inside the cover, each featuring the object. Tibor felt so 'unworthy' of it that when he had asked to be photographed with it, he couldn't bring himself to actually hold it.

As it turned out The Police later rejected Storm's picture featuring Jody for being 'too threatening'.

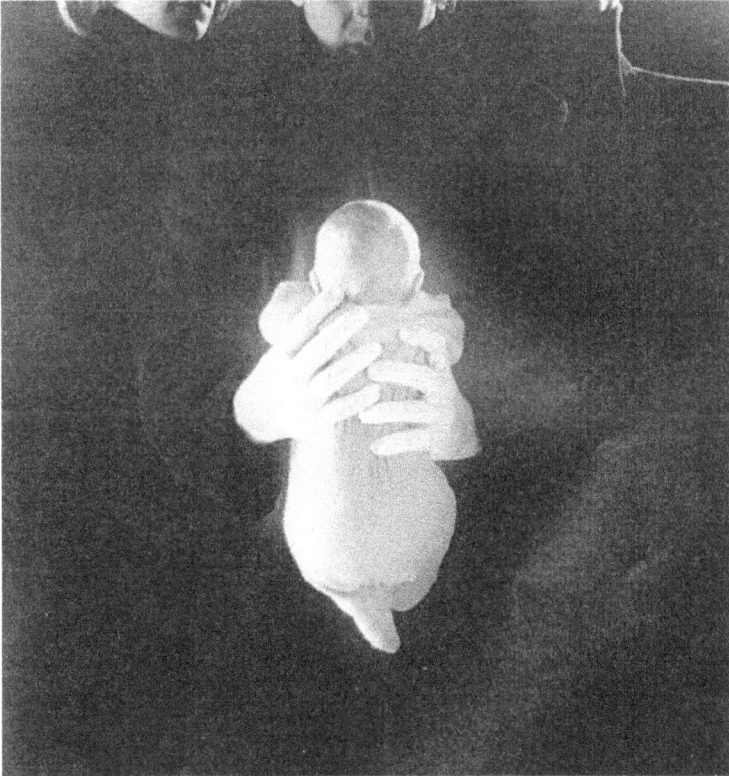

Storm holding Jody for The Police project

New Directions

Six months later Libby took a job in a bookshop in Hampstead and Tibor looked after Jody during the day. In a way Tibor was feeling a bit lost, not knowing where his drumming career was going, if anywhere. He knew he had to do something, but he had no idea what that might be.

Jody was growing up and Tibor was getting tired of living in London with all the noise coming up from the street - road drills, milk bottles, cars vandalized and stolen and all the racket from the pub across the road.

Tibor thought it was time that they moved on and into the country. Libby agreed. They started looking at estate agent advertisements and were very taken by some 'ultra-modern houses in a lakeside setting' called Pinewood Park in Farnborough, Hampshire on the M3 and not far from London. The houses were of typical new estate build. When the estate agent showed them round they were more interested in the location rather than the house itself. They bought an end of terrace house with the help of a loan from Libby's mother. The deal was quickly completed and they moved in. Jody was just one year old.

Behind the house was a vast army training ground with forests and a beautiful lake. The family used to walk there often even though it was Ministry of Defence property. In the beginning it was perfect until they were woken one night by the sound of gunfire and heavy explosions. The army was practicing, as they had every right to do, and they did this about once a week. There were flares, machine guns and even artillery fire. They wondered if they had made the right decision, leaving the noise of the city and moving into this! But they got used to it and it never lasted for very long - the MOD budget had limits!!!

Because they lived on an end of terrace house they had just one immediate neighbour. There was a narrow alleyway before the next run of houses started. When they moved there in 1981 they had a single man living immediately next to them on the right called Brian. He was a very quiet, educated guy and he worked in computers. Next to him lived a character called Gary. He was an extremely gifted artist, who painted incredibly good pictures. He was also a drummer and had his own kit in the house. A couple of doors from him lived a pilot, Martin, his wife and their two young children. Martin was a kind of hero figure to Tibor. Firstly, he was an airline pilot and was very impressive and knowledgeable. He had a big ginger beard, like a very British-Greek God. It was an honour for Tibor to become friends with someone like this. Martin flew as a co-pilot for a small outfit at Fairoaks Airport. He moved on later when he got a better job with a Birmingham-based airline called Birmingham Executive Airways or Birmex. Initially he was a co-pilot there too, and soon after he moved away from Pinewood Park. Then he became a Captain fairly quickly. This airline later changed its name to Birmingham European Airways. By the time Tibor himself joined BEA, having been heavily influenced by him, Martin had moved on elsewhere to flying jets.

Their neighbour Brian also moved to be replaced by a couple called George and Janet, who were about 35. Tibor and Libby didn't like them. They had two large noisy dogs and George was in the habit of playing unreasonably loud music at inappropriate times. The paper-thin walls didn't help. Tibor and George had a few verbal skirmishes. On one particular evening he wound Tibor up really badly. First, Tibor knocked on the wall so hard that his hand went through the plaster! George knocked back but kept on with the noisy music. Tibor felt that he had to protect his family so he went outside, opened George's external utility cupboard and flicked his mains electricity off. This did the trick and everything went silent. George came out. He didn't hit Tibor, which is what he expected, but they had a huge screaming match which eventually fizzled out. They went to bed exhausted.

Gary and Tibor hatched a plan to deal with George. They agreed that if he played loud music again they would use their weapons, drumming separately but at the same time. They never worked out what piece they were going to play unlike the perfectly synchronised gigs of Phil Collins and Chester Thompson the drummers of Genesis. Their efforts would be a lot less pleasant. But as it happened, George decided to wind his neck in after the last incident. Not long after this the couple moved on and were replaced by a pair of young morons called Steve and Christine. They had two yappy dogs the size of small cats.

A year or so later a funny thing happened. Tibor was working as a flying instructor at Three Counties Aeroclub at Blackbushe, when none other than George walked in. He knew that Tibor was learning to fly at the time of their skirmishes, but he didn't know what he was doing now. He came to inquire about learning to fly or at least going up for a trial lesson. Having watched and waited for the most effective moment, Tibor walked out and offered himself as his guide and instructor. George's eyes widened, turned down the offer and walked straight out! Tibor had a good laugh while he explained to the rest of the staff who the man was and why they may have lost his business.

Two years before they moved from Pinewood Park, Tibor and Libby decided to alter the kitchen/diner to make it more open-plan. They employed a neighbour from across the alleyway called Richard who was a builder, to do the work. Richard and his wife Imelda had one young daughter. While he was doing the job he mentioned that they were at the very end of the approval procedure for them to emigrate to Canada. Until the time they asked him to work for them they didn't really know him well. They had always assumed he was a conventional, hardworking guy. A box with some dope had been left out by mistake on their kitchen worktop, which Richard stumbled across one day. He then revealed to them, that he and Imelda also smoked dope. Tibor and Libby were amused and surprised. They had never considered this to be a possibility. Richard did a splendid job for them and when it came to saying goodbye he gave them a box of his leftover dope and grass as a leaving present. It was a nice touch.

Obviously they didn't want any complications with their emigration. It showed that even the people next door might not be what you perceive them to be!

As it turned out Farnborough was very much focused on aviation with the bi-annual air show at the local airport. They still hadn't much money and Tibor needed a job even though Libby was working as a part-time teacher and doing some coaching. He decided of all things that he would learn to drive a bus. He applied to the local bus company, passed the selection test, completed his training and started driving single and double-decker buses in Guildford for £6000 per year. This wasn't much even back then. He very quickly learned to hate the job! The Trevor Rabin fiasco continued to haunt him and disturb him. He still aspired to make it as a musician, not having given up trying he joined a band called Visa, based back in London. They had a singer from Belfast who sounded not unlike Phil Lynott of Thin Lizzy. Their music was punchy and energetic, but they had no management, no rudder. They rehearsed and rehearsed and eventually secured a few gigs, the best of which was at The Marquee in London where they supported a girl band called Rock Goddess. Visa's lead guitarist Mark, knew the band through friends in

London. Of course they had a girl drummer and Tibor thought she was excellent, very ballsy with loads of spirit and talent. Visa did some gigs in Edinburgh too, but they needed a break, a piece of luck but it never came their way. Visa broke up after a couple of years.

Tibor travelled to Guildford driving buses every day and sometimes had to work on the night shifts. Occasionally they had a baby-sitter and Libby would come with him at night to keep him company, sitting on the step next to him. At those times the buses were mostly empty and it was lonely work. He had to keep to the schedule and could never be early. Often he had to park up and wait for the time to pass and then move on. The most passengers he ever had on board at night were just two or three. The job started to wear him down, he could make no progress musically and he felt that this just couldn't be it.

They had another neighbour called Martin who worked for a catering company driving a van, delivering ingredients for vending machines. Martin told him that he was going to hand in his notice and wondered if Tibor wanted to take over from him. He thought that it couldn't be worse than driving a bus on shifts. He applied for the job and got it. He went out every day with boxes of goods all over the south of England, going as far as Portsmouth, Hayling Island, Reading and Oxford. He got to know the area well and was pleased that he didn't have to do the run into London like some of the others. Tibor completed his deliveries as quickly as he could to get home to Libby and Jody. Sometimes this backfired on him, as the company would give him another huge load to deliver to Frimley Hospital. Tibor was however much happier in this job.

On 12th August 1982 Tibor and Libby were married. They realized that they didn't need to do this since they were perfectly settled, happy with the status quo but they decided to do it for Jody's sake. They appreciated that it would make life much simpler for him. They informed their families but didn't want to make a big thing of it - no church wedding! While they were setting things up a couple of friends, Di and Pete came to stay for a few days, transiting to their new lives in Australia . They arranged a Registry Office wedding in Aldershot. So Di and Pete became their witnesses. Jody, who was now almost two, went with them. Although he wasn't aware of it, it was a significant day for him as he would cease to be a bastard! Libby wore a bright pink boiler suit and a white pair of clogs. Tibor wore a black T-shirt and a pair of turquoise jeans. The ceremony took just 15 minutes and then they were man and wife.

Chapter Twelve
Learning to Fly

Jody was growing up and Tibor was fast approaching 30. He realized that he badly needed to find another interest in his life, another challenge. He hit on the idea of taking flying lessons. If nothing else he wanted to know what it would feel like to be flying in a light aircraft. They lived close to Blackbushe Airport and he drove over there with Libby one day. It was a small airport but there were two flying schools. One was very old looking with equally old Cessnas. There was another much newer school with low wing, more stylish Grummans. They went in there and were met by an engaging man, who turned out to be an instructor at the school. His name was Peter Diggin.

After a casual chat with Peter, Tibor decided to book a lesson, but not on that day as they'd been to the pub earlier. He'd had a couple of pints, which had actually given him the courage to even go to the school. Peter said he could book him in and that if he took three lessons in one, it would work out cheaper for him. The first lesson would be a trial but it would count towards the 35 flying hours, which he needed to clock up in order to obtain his pilot's license. Tibor took to Peter immediately and later found out that he had a marvellous sense of humour. So here he was living out another of his dreams - something he'd always felt he had in him from the time of his blue shirt and the Boeing 707, which he had explored all those years ago with Shraga.

Tibor turned up for his trial lesson and Peter briefed him with a model plane then showed him round the aircraft they were to fly in, which was a Grumman Cheetah AA5A. He told Tibor that he would take the aircraft up and fly towards Basingstoke, their 'playground'. After he had explained to Tibor some of the basics of flying, Peter took off 'pattering' to Tibor through the process and the plane climbed away beautifully. Tibor certainly didn't understand everything Peter was telling him, but he listened intently and did his best to comprehend and take it all in. Over Basingstoke Tibor took over the controls, turned left, turned right, put the aircraft in a climb and felt that this was something he could really get used to. They flew back to Blackbushe and Peter landed it. The flight lasted about 30 minutes, which is normal for a trial lesson. Then the next lesson was put in the diary. Tibor had to make a decision about the options open to him. Either pay lesson by lesson, or pay for the whole course up front at a cheaper rate. At the end he paid for the whole course in advance, which cost £2500. With a Private Pilot's License (PPL) he could hire a plane and fly even as far as France. An exciting prospect! His low feelings about failing to make it in the music business just drifted away. He felt uplifted and the course really began.

Every pilot will remember his or her first solo flight and Tibor is no exception. It's an achievement that marks a real separation from Earth. It's the first time that a pilot goes flying without any supervision. It's a big and important day. By this time Tibor had completed some 15 hours of dual training and his first solo was to be set up for the next day, based on the previous day's session, when he had performed enough 'touch and goes' without any input from Peter.

Tibor would fly two circuits: taking off, landing then a non-stop rolling take off and a full stop landing and if Peter was still happy he would send Tibor off on his own. On the day of the solo flight he arrived at the school with Libby. She wanted to see him fly his first solo. Tibor and Peter went through their briefing and took off. The weather was perfect with light winds and good visibility and they flew a couple of circuits. Then Peter said he was getting out. He pushed the canopy back, clambered out, wished Tibor good luck and left the plane.

Excited and shitting bricks at the same time Tibor closed the sliding perspex canopy of the Grumman. He taxied to the power check position next to the runway and went through his checklist one item at a time. When he was satisfied that everything was good he reported to Blackbushe tower: 'ready for departure'.

Once he had permission to go he lined up on Runway 26 towards the west. Then he put on full power, checked the swing, keeping the aircraft straight with the rudder. He accelerated to approximately 60 knots, eased back on the control column and the plane climbed away, but this time at a markedly faster vertical rate than at any time before, because Peter was missing! He glanced at the empty seat to his right. He was used to a lesser rate of climb with the weight of two people on board, but now the plane was climbing like a 'homesick angel'! He levelled off at a thousand feet and carried out the after take-off checks. Then he turned left into the crosswind leg and left again downwind. He completed the downwind and pre-landing checks and reported to the tower, 'downwind'. He then turned left again onto 'base leg' extending some flap, starting to slow down and descending at the same time. Next, he made a left turn to 'finals' and reported it. The control tower responded that he was clear to land on Runway 26 with a surface wind of 290 degrees at eight knots. A crosswind from the right! Now he had to keep the nose right of the centre-line and into the light wind, otherwise he would be drifting to the left. It takes a bit of practice not to be tempted to head straight towards the runway, but to the right of it. But by doing this, his track over the ground was perfect and straight towards the runway, which was to his left in the windscreen. Next he selected final flap, did his landing checks and decelerated to threshold speed. He came over the perimeter fence at some 30 feet then continued his descent to about five feet from the ground. He closed the throttle and, just as the plane started the final sink, he gave it a little left rudder to straighten the nose down the runway. He checked back on the control column and touched down on the main gears, slightly left of the markings. Gently breaking, he slowed down to walking pace and took the next turning left and off the runway. He was so very, very happy. He felt a great sense of tension flow out of him. He pushed the canopy open as he taxied into the parking position. He shut down and completed the shutdown checks. As the propeller stopped he jumped out of the aircraft and into Libby's arms. Peter was already busy with the paperwork. He smiled, shook Tibor's hand and gave him a First Solo Certificate and a small pair of cheap 'golden', yet so very valuable, wings - to put on his shirt! Tibor felt he was now well on the way to becoming a private pilot. He had survived his first solo! Wow.

Tibor went through the rest the course, learning more about flying with Peter, at times going solo again and eventually completing a long cross-country navigation exercise on his own. This involved landing at two separate airfields and obtaining a signature from each of their towers. Peter then declared that Tibor was ready to go for his General Flying Test (GFT), which he would have to do with someone other than Peter. He also had to sit some written exams, which was a bit of a challenge as he hadn't sat an exam since he was 17 and he was now nearly 30. He had never done well in written exams but, as he found out, these writtens were not all that difficult. The exams related to meteorology, airframes and engines and the theory of flight. He passed them all with great relief. Then he was sent for the GFTs to Biggin Hill, an unfamiliar airport. It took two goes, after a partial pass, but on the second attempt he completed it all. Wooooshhh!

During this time he never lost his passion for drumming. He had a kit at home and played often but he had no plans to join a band as flying was now his passion. With his private pilot's license he could only fly recreationally, not for 'hire or reward'. He started to think seriously about changing this. He took his family and friends for flights sometimes accepting cash payments to help cover the cost of fuel. Even back then to hire a light plane worked out at about £80 per hour. It wasn't cheap. He flew short hops like going to the Isle of Wight and back. He took Libby, Jody and Bill up and even his mother.
He flew as far as France to Le Touquet to bring back some Beaujolais Nouveau and fresh baguettes!

Róza had visited the UK to meet Libby and then again a number of times after Jody was born. Libby and Tibor had paid for her travels and she had stayed with them for a month at a time. She was very proud of her grandson. Sometime after Tibor had passed his flying test, Róza came to stay with them in Farnborough. It was while she was with them this time that Tibor offered to take her flying.

She loved it! During the flight he had explained to her what he was doing and why. She was very impressed and trusted him totally. He realized on that flight that he could actually teach flying. This vision needed to be followed through and his mind was made up. Flying for a living was what he now wanted to do and felt he could achieve. He would train to be an instructor later, albeit after a stint in the offices of Blackbushe School of Flying for a year.

Tibor hadn't expected that his mother would enjoy flying with him as much as she did, nor that she would like smoking dope! She had always been a cigarette smoker and she occasionally had a hit on a joint. Róza was nearly 70 and Tibor was amazed that she enjoyed the feeling of being lightly stoned with them.

Getting Up to Tricks

While they were living at Pinewood Park and when Jody was about three or four he used to play outside in front of the houses. There was a secure square without traffic, where young children could play together safely. There was a wooden fence with a gate behind the houses and gardens, which led from the estate to the woods and the lake beyond. Ideally this gate was locked and only the adjoining properties, some 15 or so, had keys. It provided some security from would-be intruders coming from the woods. More importantly it kept the children inside the estate and out of the woods and away from the lake.

The fence on the left side of Tibor and Libby's house was in a bad state of repair. Those properties were separated from Tibor's run of houses by a narrow alleyway leading from the front of the houses alongside the length of their garden fence towards the gate to the woods. As far as Tibor was concerned this section of fence was not their responsibility. Almost all the families had children so it was in their best interest to have it mended. They were private properties so the council wasn't going to conduct the repairs.

Tibor came up with a cheeky idea that he never thought would work. He used an electric typewriter and typed out eight identical copies of a letter, mentioning the state of the fence, which by this time was almost flat on the ground, pointing out that it was a danger for all their children, who could get through to the woods and even to the lake. Tibor proposed that on the following Sunday at 2.00pm they should all meet up with tools to pick up the broken fence and fix it. He put these letters through the letter-boxes, each one 'signed' by the next-door neighbour. He delivered them at night and waited to see what would happen.

To his utter amazement on the following Sunday at 2pm a small gathering assembled to the left of the rear gardens. Tibor and Libby watched from an upstairs window wondering what would happen next. They couldn't stop laughing. All the residents were there with their tools. Much to Tibor's satisfaction they picked up and fixed the fence. The prank was productive and amusing at the same time. Whenever Tibor bumped into his neighbours over the next few days he mentioned how impressed he was by their community spirit! And the children were safer too.

Not long after his fence mending prank, he came up with another truly awful idea! He had noticed that many of the houses on the 1970s estate had double-glazed UPVC leaded windows as if the owners thought they were living in an Elizabethan cottage or a manor house. It was absurd and very pretentious. All the houses had single-glazed windows, thin walls and they were very close together.

It occurred to Tibor that these people should be made aware of their pretentious behaviour. So he devised another letter, which purported to come from the 'ugliest house' on the estate near its centre. He tore a picture from the Yellow Pages of a huge triple-sectioned bay window, which was double-glazed and with leaded windows. He photocopied it onto A4 sheets, positioning it to the top centre of the sheet. Underneath he typed Leaded Windows Society in red, so that it looked authentic. Under this 'heading' he then notified the recipients that a huge inaugural party was to be held at this particular house on a forthcoming Sunday afternoon, urging everyone with leaded windows to turn up where a great time to was to be had, including a raffle, and some stunningly awful prizes! The top 'prize' was be a free weekend down on the south coast in one of the member's static caravans(!), boasting - guess what... leaded windows! He posted the letters to all the houses with leaded windows that qualified. Sadly they were away on the specified Sunday so they never knew how many people turned up at the ugly house with their 'invitations' or how its occupants handled the party they never knew about. But just thinking about it was funny and gave Tibor some satisfaction if it caused the pretentious window owners a moment to think about themselves and their silly, posy, frilly, chintzy ways.

Tibor's final prank came later in the mid 90s, which was to do with Junk Mail, which everyone seemed to hate. Tibor came up with a way to have his revenge. Every day they would get a handful of this stuff through the post but then something dawned on him. He realized that the reply paid envelopes could be utilized against the very source that polluted everyone's doorstep. He took these envelopes and mixed up the junk mail from one to the other and posted them back. It was very therapeutic but more and more junk mail kept coming and he looked forward each day to doing his thing with them, laughing along with Libby. He was reading a Stephen King book at the time and he came across a character called *Fucko The Clown*. Tibor decided he could be this character in the junk mail world. He could become this warrior, this junk mail fiend. He printed up lots of clown pictures from the internet and added these to his junk mail mailings, with the caption Fucko The Clown. He wasn't mad, just needed his revenge. He wondered how the companies involved responded to these mailings. Junk mail has all but dried up now and Tibor wonders how much his campaign contributed to this!

Up Against JDS

Once Tibor had passed his PPL flight test in 1985, he tried to get a job in the flying school office. BSF the school at Blackbushe was one of a group. There were others at Biggin Hill, Elstree and at Denham. John Dow Smith was in charge of the Blackbushe arm of the group and Tibor approached him for a job. He didn't like JDS (as he was known) and found him to be a nasty piece of work. Tibor kept on asking and eventually JDS took him on as Operations Manager and he joined the school. He left the van driving job and started at Blackbushe on about the same rate of pay. The work was much more interesting though. He manned the office, took bookings, scheduled lessons and allocated instructors to students. He did the accounts and he cashed up, working single-handedly. Sometimes in the afternoons a school boy called Nicholas came in to help out but basically Tibor ran the office.

Eventually Tibor fell out with JDS. The dispute was around a request from one of their instructors called Gary, who wanted to fly an aircraft in the annual, very prestigous Schneider Trophy race on the Isle of Wight. Gary had himself asked JDS well in advance, if he could take the weekend off to take part in the event. Weekends of course are the busiest of times at any flying school and JDS immediately told him that it was out of the question. Later Gary asked Tibor if he could cover for him and told him that he would leave a message on the school answer machine in the morning saying that he was sick and couldn't come in to work, in order to attempt to avert potential blame falling on Tibor's shoulders. It was forbidden to instruct, if unwell. He asked Tibor to reschedule his lessons. On the Friday afternoon before the race, Gary climbed into a non-school, private aircraft belonging to his friend Dennis, with whom he was going to do the competition. Unfortunately he was spotted by Stewart, one of the managers of the airport, who always knew too much! Stewart called JDS at Biggin Hill and told him what he had just seen. On Saturday JDS rang Tibor, as per routine at Blackbushe and asked if all the instructors were in. Tibor of course told him that Gary had left a message that he was sick and wouldn't be coming in. JDS told Tibor to call Gary again. He knew what he was doing. Tibor realized that the game was up and that JDS wouldn't mess around. He was a ruthless man. Tibor rang JDS and told him that he 'could not get hold of Gary'. JDS said he would take care of it. Tibor sat down and typed out a resignation letter. At the same time JDS picked up an aircraft from Biggin Hill and set off for Blackbushe. Tibor had a friend in the control tower called Paul, who phoned Tibor to alert him that an aircraft was approaching from the direction of London and that it was JDS.

After he had landed JDS came into the office and calmly told Tibor to come upstairs. He asked for an explanation. Tibor didn't even attempt one. He told JDS that he knew he would be fired and handed over his resignation letter. JDS was stunned and told Tibor that he done the decent thing and would be given a few weeks to find another job.

He went home and told Libby, feeling awful and yet relieved. They agreed after some discussion that it would be the right time for him to begin his Instructor's Course. He found that the best place to do this was at High Wycombe. There he was allocated to John Loveridge, the 'instructor's instructor', who was an ex-VC10 captain. John had been an instructor for many years and was everyone's choice if they could get him. He was a small man, who initially appeared to be a miserable guy. He was a genius in his field though and he soon warmed towards Tibor, who also took to John. The course cost more than a basic flying course and the pay as instructor wasn't going to be that good, but it's what he wanted to do.

John took Tibor through the ground school and practical flying course. It was a mandatory 35 hour course and he chose to add a further qualification at the same time, to instruct students to fly relying solely on instruments. This was called an IMC rating and Tibor thought it useful to have under his belt. John and Tibor went flying daily, but at times he was paired up with another student and they were required to practice the skills by instructing each other, both in the classroom and in the air. For example, Tibor 'taught' his partner how to fly a climbing turn and his partner 'taught' Tibor how to fly a descending turn, both using the appropriate 'patter'.

John told Tibor that part of the course involved having to control a spinning aircraft. He explained that if a student let an aircraft get into a spin Tibor had to be able to rescue it. If he couldn't do that they would both be dead! There are two elements to be taught here. One is the type of entry to and causes of a spin, the other is the all-important recovery from it. On the day they went out to do this exercise Tibor was worried. He had never favoured aerobatics, or the thought of it, and going into a spin was right on the edge of this. John demonstrated the first spin. Then it was Tibor's turn.

An aircraft in a spin feels like the machine is out of control, as at that moment it's not really flying, but turning on its own vertical axis at an extremely fast rate, rapidly losing height. There are different circumstances from which an aircraft could enter a spin. With a *power on* spin the pilot has to raise the nose of the aircraft quite high allowing the airspeed to decay and then apply plenty of rudder, turning the plane momentarily on its back until it starts spinning. This type of entry to the spin is complicated by the fact that the propeller is spinning as well. With a *power off* spin it is less vicious an entry, as the pilot doesn't have to raise the nose as high. When an aircraft goes into a spin the pilot has to recognise which way its spinning - left or right - and then use the prescribed technique to bring it back under control and ease it out of the dive. This isn't natural to a person and there are many different rules to abide by. He worked with John and gained confidence rapidly. Later he practiced spinning with his partner too and they both amazingly ended up really enjoying it!

He travelled to High Wycombe daily. On one occasion whilst there he fell into conversation with a girl, who was learning to fly. It turned out that she was Hungarian and, what's more, from Budapest! She invited him to visit her there next time he was in that city. Later that year he went there with Libby and they were introduced to her mother who had recently retired from Hungarian television. She asked him how he had become a pilot and he told her that story amongst others from his past. She was most impressed and said that a film should be made about his life. This was a moment when Tibor was made to recognize that his life's story may well be of interest to others.

Tibor finished his course, parted from John for the last time and then had to take the final flying test with a 'Panel Examiner'. These examiners were highly experienced pilots and there were only a handful of them in the country. His examiner was called Laurie Adlington. He was ex-RAF with a classic grey-white aviator's handlebar moustache and was also the Chief Flying Instructor at the other flying school at Blackbushe called Three Counties Aero Club. He could fly anything and everything *and* extremely well at that. Fortunately Laurie couldn't have been closer than right on the same airfield where Tibor learnt to fly and worked for a year previously. He knew that Tibor originated from the 'opposition' on the field but he was still happy to take him on for the test.

Laurie told Tibor that the task would be to brief him on a particular subject in the class-room and then 'instruct' the same topic while they were airborne. Tibor went through a lesson using a blackboard, 'chalk and talk' style, and Laurie asked student-like questions. When that was completed they took to the air. Luckily the weather was good and up they went with Tibor talking him through the lesson, feeling increasingly confident as time went on. Laurie was his first 'student' and it felt like it was going the right way.

They landed and Laurie turned to him as they were taxiing in saying, 'I guess now you want a job'. Tibor was taken aback and asked, 'so did I pass then?' and Laurie confirmed that he had and was indeed offering him a job in a rather dry, but humorous way. They completed the formalities and sent the paperwork off to the Civil Aviation Authority. His accreditation arrived in due course. Laurie told Tibor that he wanted him to start with some trial lessons to slowly ease him in. A couple of weeks later he was called in by the Flying School for his first three trial lessons on a busy Saturday as an Instructor. As is usual in these trial lessons, the students were completely blown away by the experience. Tibor was equally elated to have successfully come through this first exciting day in his new job. Soon after this he was taking on students for the whole course. There were four or five instructors at the school but Tibor became very popular and started to build up quite a following. He was confident, warm and easy-going and they liked that. Students could relate to him. Some of the other instructors were perhaps more formal and less 'colourful'. The pay was poor but he was kept very busy, adding to his own flying time in his logbook, but now not having to pay for it himself! When the weather was bad and the students still came in, Tibor did ground school work with each of them. On good weather days, before every flight he held a classroom briefing and then they flew for 45 or 50 minutes. It was a good life!

At around this time he noticed that some of his colleagues were leaving to go to college to study to become Airline Pilots. Tibor had never considered this as an option before, but now he began to think seriously about it as well. He realized that many people only viewed instructing as a stepping stone into commercial flying. If you weren't rich, the only way to get into Aviation College was by becoming an instructor first, gaining log book time, because you needed 700 hours of flying time to be even taken on a course. He borrowed some books and notes and read up on the Commercial Pilot's License (CPL) course. Because he loved flying he was able to apply himself. Reading these course note books was quite tortuous as they were meant to be only an accompaniment to college lectures, but he persevered. He had always been interested in aero engines right from his schooldays in Haifa and he was captivated by the theory of flight. It would be a new and exciting direction for him to take in life. Somehow it would be comparable to making it in the music business and if he got the license he could start to earn some really good money. It felt right to try and if it didn't work he knew he could fall back on flying instruction. Again he discussed things with Libby and again she agreed that he should go for it. He was now 35 years old.

Name Games

During early life in Israel Tibor felt most uncomfortable with his Hungarian surname, so he had decided to change it to Shahar, which means 'dawn' in Hebrew. This sounded better there than Vásárhelyi. Then having settled in England, he again felt out place with his

Israeli name. One of his students at the Three Counties Aero Club was a London solicitor and Tibor asked him how difficult it would be for him to change his name. The solicitor explained that it was not a difficult process. It would be done by deed poll and he could choose whatever name he liked. He immediately concluded that it should be January. It was the obvious choice since it was already Libby's surname. On his next flying lesson the solicitor brought in the paperwork, which required Tibor's signature, and the process began. It was soon completed and he became **Tibor January**.

About 5 years earlier when they married, Libby became Mrs Shahar and now she became Mrs January and Jody's name changed likewise. Tibor and Libby laughed when they thought of the likely puzzlement at her bank - how Miss January could have become Mrs Shahar but then Mrs January! Did she marry her brother, her father?

Chapter Thirteen
Becoming a Commercial Pilot

At the age of 35, Tibor decided to go for the airline pilot course - somewhat a late start in life. The notes he was reading up till now were not good enough and he enrolled on a Correspondence Course with a college in Kent. Tibor decided to do the course if just as an interim measure before he attended a college course in person! He had little confidence in his academic abilities and in this way, he hoped to give himself a 'flying start'! He completed the correspondence course and then registered with a college in London known as CAS - the Civil Aviation Studies College, at the London City Polytechnic. It's now called The London Metropolitan University now. It was a three month course covering the Technical side of flying, Performance and Navigation. If he passed this written section he would be half way towards attaining his CPL. It was 1988 and Jody was eight. Before he started the course the family took a holiday in Florida. They had the time of their lives, visiting Epcot Centre, Wet and Wild and Disney World and

Jody loved it. It was a great thing to do before he knuckled down to his studies, which he was not looking forward to.

Storm (Libby's 'ex') had a tiny spare room in his flat in Belsize Park and he kindly offered it to Tibor during his study period in London. Storm was not there much, but Bill lived there. Bill was a young man by this time and he had formed a band called Bay of Pigs. Bill was in and out overnight like a cat. Sometimes he had friends in, which was OK with Tibor. It was his home after all. Tibor started attending college and it was very daunting. The hardest element was called Performance-A. He was taught for example how to calculate the maximum allowable take-off weight, at the prevailing conditions on a particular runway, when one of the engines fail just at the moment of rotation on a three engine jet passenger/cargo aircraft or when two engines fail on a four engine plane. The examples were worked out on either a Boeing 747 or a Tristar. The subject demanded a high degree of accuracy. Schemes were worked out using a series of dots on special graph paper, which was considered the best way to give an accurate answer to a problem. It was a nightmare. It was virtually impossible to produce a totally accurate answer just as it was to understand the whole subject.

There were other subjects, which he took to more easily. Meteorology was one of these. He could grasp the topic. It was logical and it made sense to him. In one of the exams he was required to predict what the weather would be at a particular position and time by tracking how various fronts were progressing using all the skills he had been taught. Navigation was however more of a nightmare. In Tibor's flying experience this subject differed greatly from theory to practice. The course would end with a two day, 16 exam frenzy! Failing three subjects would have meant re-taking the whole 16 again! If he had had to retake the whole course he would have been overwhelmed. Many students did get caught in that hellish cycle and never managed to pass. After failing the lot three times, it wasn't possible to sit the exams again. All this created an enormous amount of pressure on all the candidates.

One Thursday morning during the course at around 6:00am, Storm's phone rang. Storm was in the USA and Bill was asleep, so Tibor answered the phone, which was in Storm's bedroom. It was Libby and she told him that she just had a call from Israel and that sadly his mother had died unexpectedly. He couldn't believe it. A few weeks previously she had been admitted to hospital with some minor problem, which hadn't been considered serious. He didn't know what to do next. He heard a key turn in the lock in the flat's front door! In walked Storm, who was very surprised to find Tibor in his bedroom, still sitting on his bed wearing only his underwear. He explained to Storm what had just happened and Storm was equally shocked by the news. Tibor didn't know what to do for the best - whether he should drop out of the course and go to Israel, which in a way he could have used as an excuse to escape the study pressure, or continue with the course. After some soul searching, considering that his mother surely would have wanted him to carry on the path he had set himself, he made the decision to go into college that day. Soon after this he heard from his relatives that they would take care of the funeral arrangements and bury his mother. Having been in college all day on returning to the flat that evening he found Storm sitting in the same place on his own bed, looking deep in thought. Incredibly, he informed Tibor that *his* own father had died suddenly that very same day. What a sad coincidence to share! Storm wasn't close to his father, but it was still a loss to be contended with. Through all this emotional turmoil Tibor struggled hard and managed to complete his homework, went into college on

Friday and then, with some relief, went home exhausted for the weekend.

When he finally sat his exams, he achieved a partial pass. He considered that a great achievement in itself. He then re-sat the two outstanding modules and this time he achieved the full pass! With this in hand he'd completed his CPL written exams. He thought the flying side must be easier but, as it turned out, it wasn't!

He chose to go to a flying school in Bournemouth called SFT, which had a good reputation. He had a battered old Honda Accord and it was a long drive from home, which was too much to take on on a daily basis. He rented a cheap room in the ugliest part of Bournemouth in a private house, intending to go to flying school every day. This lasted just one single, sad and lonely night! The next day he packed up and left the accommodation, knowing that the daily drive home wouldn't be half as bad as it had seemed just a day earlier.

SFT worked on a conveyer belt system, taking on three new students every week. On his first day he was grouped with two other students. They were both ex-RAF pilots - one had been flying a Tornado and the other was a Red Arrows Captain. Tibor felt he was in tough, mismatched company with his background of flying single-engined Cessnas and Cherokees. He soon became aware that the school was not too clever in their grouping of students and he quickly started to feel left behind. They talked about aircraft systems he'd never even heard of, but without prior introduction, like cross-feeding from one fuel tank to the opposite engine. It's a complex procedure and the RAF guys knew all about this already. It was daunting for Tibor and he had to steel himself to carry on, but he did.

Before he could start to study he had to be Type-Rated (the 1179 test) on the aircraft type he would be training and later be tested on. He was to use the twin-engined Piper Aztec. They flew as a group of maybe four or five on board and were given two days to become familiar with the aircraft. Then they started to learn the rules of accurate instrument flight on a professional level. After mixing visual with instrument flying the instructor then placed panels in the cockpit. The instructor could see out but the student could see nothing except the instruments. They had to fly straight and level at a particular speed then perform turns, climbing turns and descending turns. It was extremely demanding work as single crew and required a high degree of concentration. The next part of the process was to incorporate navigation and using the radio. They would navigate to an airport and be required to make an instrument let down using ILS - the instrument landing system. The task was made harder because the aircraft was not properly sealed and the engines made a lot of noise. Rainwater got in to the cabin and Tibor describes it as 'agricultural flying'!

The upshot was that Tibor had to pass the Instrument Rating test, which is the most demanding of flying tests to conquer. The test involves a full briefing to be received from a CAA Flying Unit (CAAFU) examiner dressed in full airline uniform, who would then join the aircraft just before engine start and the test would commence. After a visual take off he would fully close the screens and Tibor would then be required to demonstrate his ability to cope with an engine failure, which the examiner would simulate by throttling back an engine. Subsequently navigation, liaison with Air Traffic Control and an approach at a Channel Island airport, followed by a single engine go-round, then a return to land had to be performed. Partly due to the difficulty of the highest of standards required from a candidate and in part due to SFTs lack of personal attention his first attempt was a failure. The second attempt was also a failure. Then Tibor decided to take a break from the Instrument Rating and focused on another task, the General Flying Tests (GFTs).

This next part of the course took him to Goodwood to fly a single engine Cherokee for some hours with an instructor, extending his instrument navigation skills. Then followed another flight test with another CAA examiner. On that day Tibor flew an aircraft to Bournemouth in order to brief and then fly with an examiner from the CAAFU. Tibor liked the examiner. He was friendly and supportive. He briefed Tibor well before they started and he put up the screens. He instructed him to fly to some specific coordinates and after a while he removed the screens and Tibor looked down and saw the Cerne Abbas man with his enormous erection carved in the landscape! The examiner laughed with satisfaction as the candidate has spotted his intended target. A short time later a friend sent him a post-card of the Cerne Abbas man with a note on the back which read,' I bet you never wanted to see a man's erection so much as you did on that day'.

During his time away from SFT and the Instrument Rating he had time and energy to reflect and consider how to return to this seemingly impossible challenge. It became clear to him that SFT had played a significant part in his double failure. They hadn't considered pairing candidates suitably, mainly by backgrounds and experience, nor had they given enough personal attention to the individual's differing needs. He then constructed a letter to this effect and sent it to SFT's management, suggesting that they were to blame and requesting some kind of recompense. The fees were very high at £300 a flying hour and SFT were in a comfortable position with a continuous full house of students. It was an endless money pit.

SFT, to Tibor's enormous surprise, conceded to his points and in return offered him a quota of free simulator instruction and some free flying time to get him finally to the required standard. Eventually the day came when Captain Dick Snell (CAAFU) was the man on duty to take Tibor's final flight test and to give him his long awaited PASS!!!

In the summer of 1989 at last Tibor submitted his plethora of paperwork to the Civil Aviation Authority and a few days later he received in the post the much desired blue plastic covered Commercial Pilot's License. He had done what he set out to do and he had achieved his goal!

Chapter Fourteen

Airline Pilot

Tibor had been in touch with an airline called Birmingham European Airways a year and a half before he had finished all his courses. The company had no connection with the old BEA. He and his mate Gary, the instructor from Blackbushe, now an airline pilot himself, who previously worked at this company, flew into Birmingham in a light aircraft where he introduced Tibor to Captain Dave Roberts, the Chief Pilot of the airline, for an early interview. He took a liking to Tibor and before parting that day, asked to be kept informed of his progress. Tibor had kept in touch. He obviously wasn't the only pilot on the look-out for a job, but this early contact with Dave proved very useful, as he was consequently offered a job with a start date in January of 1990. This was a great relief for them as Libby had been having a slightly difficult time at the private school where she had been teaching for the last couple of years. The headmaster, an ex-Colonel imposed difficult rules and restrictions on his teaching staff. Libby was ready to move on. Without Libby's help Tibor acknowledges that he would never have gained his license, but now they had a clear path ahead of them. Jody was nearly 10. They had to think of moving from Farnborough up into the Midlands to be near Birmingham. He didn't want to commute huge distances. They decided that they should have a look at properties for rent in the area around half an hour's drive from the airport initially while they looked for something to buy.

The Bushe Pilots

Just before they moved from Pinewood Park to the Midlands, Blackbushe School of Flying organized a party and they wanted a band. The party was to be held next to the army base behind their house at the far end of the lake. There was a Water Ski club and a bar for the army and club members, with well discounted beer prices. Tibor used to go there occasionally with one of his best mates of those times, Peter Eastwood, who was an ace single barefoot water-skier and was even featured in the film *Spies Like Us*! Tibor remembers one Sunday afternoon that he and Peter had eight pints each, sitting outside the clubhouse in the sun. They both slowly became very drunk. They were so far gone that on the way back round the lake they stopped at a beautiful barn-like pub called The Mead Hall to have 'one for the road'! Even in this state they were served - unbelievably!

Peter was a mobile car mechanic. Tibor had contacted him after seeing his ad in the local paper, when their old Honda Accord had a problem. Pete turned up with his van full of tools. He was a big, strong guy and an ex-army instructor with a voice to boot! He was not to be argued with, but he had a heart of gold! He asked Tibor what he did for a living. Tibor told him that he drove a van for money and flew for fun.

Peter Eastwood and Tibor

From that day, Peter and Tibor became great friends. As a result of getting to know him, Peter decided to learn to fly too. Then, when Tibor became a flying instructor, Peter went up with him occasionally to see how it's done properly! Later he bought a Microlight aircraft, which he built himself from a kit, but unlike Tibor he didn't want to pursue flying as a career.

Peter organised the Flying School party's location, at the Water Ski Club. From amongst the flying instructors and students there were enough musicians to form a band. They decided to call themselves The Bushe Pilots! They had a professional singer called Tony Burrows, who had learnt to fly at BSF. In the past he had been in the well-known band Edison Lighthouse, which had an enormous hit single called *My Love Grows Where My Rosemary Goes* in the 1970s. They had a guy called Terry on guitar, who was an instructor and a British Airways Tristar pilot and Mike on bass, who was now doing Tibor's old job at BSF. There was also a private pilot called Dennis on guitar. In the past Tibor had taught him some instrument flying. Tibor was of course on drums. They had T-shirts printed for the event and they each had to invent a name. The picture on each black T-shirt was of Blackbushe Airport's plan view layout from above and under that he had his name 'AeroDrum' printed. The others had names like Hawkeye and Ace of the Bass. Tibor's name was far and away the most original!

They did a 60s hits repertoire and it went down amazingly well. They had a huge parachute as a backdrop and Tibor wore a wig with very long hair for the full 60s effect! It was so hot that by the end he had ditched it. They did of course do Tony's Edison Lighthouse hit. The Bushe Pilots never played again, but no one from that night will forget what a good time they had.

Just before Christmas '89 the family moved into a rented house in a tiny village in the Midlands called Weston Under Wetherley, which was about a half hour's drive from Birmingham Airport. They looked at several properties and chose one called The Ranch House. It was a single story wooden building and it stood in its own grounds. It was most unusual and they both took a liking to it straight away. The garden led into fields rising up a hillside and they were really in the country. They were pleased to get away from Farnborough and were suffused with a new optimism. They found a school for Jody and being very sociable, he settled in quickly and easily.

On 8th January 1990, Tibor started work along with three other newbies. After reporting at the airline's base, they were taken to a hotel just outside the airport for ground school to begin, to get them familiar with the technical side of the aircraft they would be flying - the British Aerospace built Jetstream 31.

Jetstream 31

The Jetstream 31 was a twin engine turboprop airplane. Turboprop means a jet engine with propellers. So no more piston engines for Tibor! It was only a 16-seater, a small aircraft, but it was progress and at this time looked enormous to him. There were two pilots with a cabin crew of one and one toilet. It wasn't British Airways although that company did have some involvement in the airline as did the Danish airline Maersk Air. The ground school lasted two weeks and the students then had to travel down to Gatwick, the headquarters of the CAA, to sit the written exam, which required a pass mark of 70% or above. They all passed. The CAA, as usual set questions designed to trip the candidate up. The golden rule was RTFQ - 'read the fucking question'! Then they progressed to actually flying the aircraft with a Type Rating Instructor and with other trainees on board. It's a cheap enough aircraft to fly and there wasn't even a simulator in existence for the type. At this stage he was a co-pilot or First Officer as they're known in the business. He passed all his tests and was immediately put on a flying roster. The schedule was worked out by the Crewing and Operations Department and they could be asked to fly up to 900 hours a year, sometimes at night and sometimes at weekends with rest days in between as prescribed by law. According to his roster he started line training, flying from Birmingham airport to other destinations, with a Line Training Captain and fare-paying passengers on board. Eventually he flew over to France and into other countries in Europe, partly to familiarize him with the way these different countries' controllers sounded over the radio. There were so many different procedures to get used to with each country doing them differently. It's a very, very steep learning curve. After several weeks he was given his final line check and was passed fit to fly a Jetstream 31 with a normal line captain. He was a happy man. He was now a fully-fledged Airline Pilot!

To start with the salary wasn't brilliant but it was a stepping stone to something bigger and better. He had started late in life and in one way would have been content to stay a co-pilot until he retired. He had no aspirations to become a captain – *yet*!

Gulfstream G1

Three months later he was called into the office and told that he was being transferred onto a slightly bigger aircraft, The Gulfstream G1. The company had three of these aircraft in their fleet. It was an American built turboprop with two engines and was a 25-seater - bigger, stronger and faster.

He went through the training routine for this aircraft and continued to fly in it for another three months. Then again he was called into the office to be told that the company was going to lease a number of Shorts 360s, known in the industry rather irreverently as the 'Shed'. Though to Tibor it was more like a skip! It was ugly, slow and cumbersome. Not a sexy airplane. None of the pilots liked it, but Tibor had no choice. He had to do as he was told. He was sent to Belfast with a number of colleagues. They stayed in a hotel in Bangor and went to the airport each day for two weeks to learn the technical side. It's a very complicated aircraft and there was a lot to learn. When the training was completed he was to go to Gatwick to sit the written exam, but when he got back to base at Birmingham he found a letter from the company in his pigeon hole, informing him that he had an invitation do a simulator selection check on a jet aircraft that the airline were bringing on line called the BAC 1-11. He knew about this acquisition but had not expected to be given the opportunity to train for it so soon. He was confused as he was almost done with the 'Shed' course, with the CAA exam still outstanding. It was puzzling. Were they giving him a choice?

Maersk Air Ltd BAC 1-11

He went upstairs to see Captain Dave Roberts to tell him how confused he was since he was due to go to Gatwick on Monday to sit his written exam on the 'Shed', but now he was being offered a chance to see how he handled the BAC 1-11 in the simulator. Dave confirmed that they wanted him to go for a selection on the 1-11 simulator and that he should nonetheless go ahead with the 'Shed' exam.

Tibor asked what would happen if he failed the 'Shed' exam and Dave told him that it 'wouldn't matter'. So he bluffed his way through the exam, not reading the questions, just filling in the answers and leaving after a few minutes much to the invigilator's surprise. In the event he achieved 43%. He failed but, as Dave had told him, it didn't matter. Much to his relief flying the 'Shed' was NOT in his destiny.

He was given a date to go down to Cranebank at Heathrow, known as 'Simulator City'. It was owned and run by British Airways with simulators and fuselage mock-ups for all their aircraft types. There he was met and briefed by Captain Rod Clarke an ex BA pilot, now working for BEA. Rod was to assess Tibor's ability in handling a jet for the first time in the very real and life-like simulator. He was to fly a short navigation exercise with different flap configurations and speeds. His flying accuracy would be tested and his airmanship decisions monitored, whilst Rod sat in the left hand seat. He finished the half hour assessment and felt like he had done well enough. They went for a coffee and a debrief. Rod told Tibor that he had successfully passed and that he would be recommending him for a 1-11 training course! He had only been with the airline for under a year and he felt he had done extremely well to have made such rapid progress.

For the training course each co-pilot was paired up with a captain and, joy of joys, he found out that he was to be paired with Dave Roberts. He was the Chief Pilot of the airline so it was a real privilege for Tibor. It was a five week course and most of the time was spent in a mock-up - The Cardboard Bomber - which was not quite a full simulator. All the instruments and switches were drawn on flat panels. There was a carousel slide-viewer in place of the windscreens. Each slide was supported by an instructor's voice, taking the students through all the technical aspects of the 1-11, subject by subject. Students could go at their own pace and, if they chose, they could repeat any elements, calling in an instructor if it was deemed necessary. There were no cut-backs here. It was top of the range! After two weeks they took an in house written exam. The next stage was 45 hours over three weeks in a full simulator at the end of which Tibor and Dave completed a final flight test and were given their Instrument and BAC 1-11 type ratings. Tibor was now cleared to fly in the real aircraft. He flew five or six circuits, take-offs and landings with a trainer, Ian Bashall smoking a never ending pipe, until he got the hang of it and produced a 'greaser of a landing'. It was 1991. Whoooshhh!

J31 G-WMCC from earlier, sadly now used for the Fire Department's fire & smoke practice at Birmingham Airport.

Chapter Fifteen
Climbing the Ladder in the Skies

Tibor loved the BAC 1-11, his very first jet and thought it was an amazingly fast and very powerful aircraft. He stayed on it for four and a half years. When the airline had taken on the 1-11 they had also taken an influx of ex-British Airways captains, who were coming up for retirement. In those days BA compulsorily retired all their pilots at the age of 55 although the law allowed flying up the age of 60. So these pilots had another five year's potential flying and they were highly experienced and sought after. It really benefited the airline to have them on board and he found himself often rostered with one of these ex-BA captains. They were each varied, but impressive characters. It was a great start for Tibor.

BEA was owned by Maersk Air, British Airways and some other investors. Eventually BA sold their shares in BEA to Maersk Air (Denmark). BEA then became Maersk Air Ltd and almost overnight all the aircraft were re-painted in British Airways livery. The company became first British Airways franchise in the UK. In point of fact, as Tibor realised, BA was just a concept. The cabin crew wore BA uniforms and when the passengers were welcomed on board, the PA announced, 'Welcome on board this British Airways flight operated by Maersk Air.' Under the cockpit outside was a small logo that stated that the aircraft was 'British Airways operated by Maersk Air'. At that time there was a British Airways base in Birmingham and BA was still flying out of Birmingham, Manchester and all other regional airports. There was an inter-airline agreement, that required Maersk Air crews from time to time to fly the Birmingham based BA aircraft, even though they were two separate airlines. There were two sizes of BAC 1-11 and on occasions it became necessary for Maersk Air crews to use the bigger BA-owned version if they had a lot of passengers. This arrangement continued for some four and a half years during which Tibor really matured in his trade.

He discovered that technically the 1-11 was far from perfect. There were problems. One of these was with the landing gear occasionally not deploying when it was needed. Tibor was never directly affected by this but some of the other crews were. Modifications were made for monitoring the system. No flight ever had to make a belly landing, but it had come close on occasions.

The 1-11 was fitted with Rolls-Royce Spey engines and they were very noisy especially on take-off. It wasn't an issue for the flight crew as the engines were way back under the tail of the aircraft. Outside the sound was deafening and the 1-11 was nicknamed 'a fuel to noise converter'. These engines were very reliable with just an occasional problem here and there. There was one instance when a captain on Tibor's flight was forced to shut one engine down on an approach to Birmingham due to increasing and uncontrollable temperature rise. They landed safely on the one remaining operating engine. Tibor recalls that the 1-11 was a British aircraft and was very strongly built. It could take a lot of abuse without bending! It was fitted with an Auto-Land system and could land entirely by itself if circumstances required it. On a normal day the crew landed the aircraft manually even if it was cloudy, descending to below the cloud base using the auto-pilot, which was coupled onto the ILS' vertical and horizontal electronic signal. The airplane picked up the signal and converted it for the auto-pilot to make adjustments. The normal procedure was to disconnect the auto-pilot when the aircraft descended beneath the cloud base, then whoever's turn it was would take over control and make the landing. But on days when the visibility was very bad - less than 550 meters - the auto-pilot had to be used to make the landing. There were two auto-pilot systems on the 1-11, the one monitoring the other, with the flight crew watching over the entire process. The aircraft could land safely in fog down to 200m visibility. Once they had touched down the captain would take over control again and the aircraft became a manual tricycle! It was a good system. Of course the crew had to engage the second auto-pilot early on in the descent because if it was left too late it wouldn't engage and the landing would have to be aborted. The 1-11 could be a little twitchy on auto-pilot so the crew had to monitor the system at all times. If the auto-pilot disconnected close to the ground for some reason on a day when it was mandatory to use it for a landing they would have to take it back up and try another approach. When they'd been around twice without being able to make a landing they would have to divert. They always had to take on enough fuel to allow for this eventuality.

While Tibor was still flying the BAC 1-11 in 1992 it became necessary to return to college for him to upgrade his CPL to the ultimate licence in aviation. This, the (ATPL) Air Transport Pilot's Licence, would eventually allow him a promotion to the position of Captain with any UK airline on any aircraft type. Without holding an ATPL one cannot become a captain in the UK. Tibor, with the airline's agreement, took all of his leave entitlement for the year and bunched it into the five weeks that the course lasted. This took place on Kidlington Airfield near Oxford. It involved commuting daily from his home. Although there was no prospect of him becoming a Captain any time soon if ever, Tibor decided to go through this necessary pain, while there wasn't too long a gap since that last load of the CPL exams. Essentially the subjects were identical in content, just certain parts were more in depth. At the end there were the exams to be taken over two days again. Thankfully a short while later the results showed that the effort wasn't wasted. He became a proud owner of the ATPL.

Chapter Sixteen
Back to Budapest with Libby

Tibor could now secure very cheap airline tickets at a 90% discount for him and his family through British Airways. He had always intended to revisit Hungary, not the people necessarily but the street where he was born and where he used to play. He wondered what it would be like to turn that corner for the first time after 23 years and to see just how much it had changed. It fascinated him and it finally felt like the right time to make that journey. He went with Libby in 1991, leaving Jody behind with a friend. Tibor needed her with him. He wanted her to share the journey.

Their landing in Hungary was an amazing experience. They passed through the same old terminal building that he'd actually departed from 23 years before! It still had the old wooden panelling that's to be expected in any East European country. The memories of the people and the uniforms just flooded back to him. He was astonished at how far behind they seemed to be - far behind Israel and England. The difference was even more apparent when they left the airport to travel into the city. The cars, the roads and the buildings were old, tired and battered. It hit Tibor hard. He felt that he had moved forward and they hadn't. Time seemed to have stood still in Budapest.

They checked into their hotel. Tibor couldn't wait to get out and go to Alig Street. He wondered again how much it would have changed over the years. When they arrived and turned that corner onto the street he saw that nothing had altered. Nothing, except that there were many more cars parked along the sides of the road. When he lived on that street there had been just half a dozen cars there and now it was full. It was very narrow and so it had been made into a one-way street. They made their way to the apartment block number 10 and stood in front of it for a while just taking it all in. It looked just like it always had done. Then he wanted to go in just to see the front door of his old flat. They found that the glazed doors leading into the building were unlocked. They entered and went up towards the second floor, first passing through the mezzanine with all the apartments' letter boxes. He checked the residents' names to see who was living in his old flat. He didn't recognize the name but right next to it what he saw utterly amazed him. There was his cousin

Ágnes's name. This was not something he had expected to
see in a million years. He was sure that after all this time
and since he had lived in two other countries she would
surely have moved on. It was a shock and he immediately
told Libby that he was completely unprepared to meet her
again so unexpectedly. He suggested that they go up to the
second floor to his old apartment door. When they got
there nothing, but nothing, had changed. The staircase, the
black and white floor tiles and his dark brown front door
with the large open-able glass panel were just the same.
Libby suggested that they at least go and take a look on the
third floor at Ágnes's door. He agreed to this but hadn't
prepared himself for what would happen next. There was
light coming through the panel of the apartment door so
there was someone at home. He just wasn't ready to make
contact. Libby felt that now was the time for him to press
the bell, but he refused. They argued quietly with hushed
voices. She said that he just *had* to press the bell. She
insisted and Tibor finally relented. He pressed the bell.

They waited, the door opened and there was his cousin
Ágnes, looking just a little older but more or less as she had
when they parted all those years ago. Not recognizing him
she asked, 'Can I help you?' Fearing possible rejection but

feeling warmly excited he said, 'OK, remember, second floor, flat number two....Tibi?' As if struck by lightning and seeing a ghost at the same time, she stood there for a moment in stunned silence. Then suddenly all the years fell away and they flew into each other's arms, both bursting into tears. They hadn't said goodbye properly and Tibor thought she might still be angry to a degree, but she wasn't. Far from it. They spoke in Hungarian so Libby couldn't understand much of what was said. She had picked up a little of the language when Róza had visited them but not much. Ágnes asked them to come in and then introduced them to her new husband, who was also called Tibor. They went through to the lounge and noticed Tibor's son, Attila, who was 17 years old. He was warm and friendly but clearly mentally handicapped. He was in a world of his own.

Very little had changed in the flat, the curtains and the chandelier were the same. In the kitchen too Tibor was amazed to see that the kitchen dresser - a stand-alone wooden cabinet with ceramic drawers and patterned glass doors - was still there. It brought back happy memories. He had always loved that cupboard. He told Ágnes how much it meant to him to see it again and she laughed. Then they sat and talked. She told him that they had tried to trace him some years ago even contacting the Red Cross, but their efforts had not produced any positive results. In fact more shockingly the Red Cross later wrongly informed them that Tibor had been killed while serving in the Israeli army. The family had been heart-broken and very saddened by this. It dawned on Tibor that this was why she looked like she was seeing a ghost when she opened the door to him and Libby. He wanted to know what had become of his second cousin and 'almost-brother' Gyuri. Ágnes told him that her son was well, married and lived nearby. She suggested that they should meet the next day. She also explained that her first husband, Gyuri's father, had died some years ago. This was partly a result of him having been attacked by some maniac with a butt of a rifle while he was serving as a pilot in the Air Force decades earlier. He had been badly injured, become epileptic and never really recovered properly.

Tibor brought her up to date with his own 23 years of personal history, including telling her that he too was now a pilot, which deeply resonated with her. She offered them some light refreshments and in particular for Tibor some homemade Goose Liver pate on bread, which like heaven, as it took him back immediately to his mother's

home cooking and all good things Hungarian. In fact
Ágnes was an outstanding cook and she catered for them
every day that they were there. She had a set of pressure
cookers like a drum kit! She cooked all the things that Tibor
ate as a little boy and the memories came flooding back
with every mouthful. Exhausted, they went back to their
hotel and Tibor could hardly sleep in expectation of the
thought of reuniting with Gyuri the next day, who was 12
when they were last together.

They returned to the flat the following day and sure
enough there was Gyuri. When they had said goodbye he
had been a little blonde stick of a boy, now he was a large
man with a beard but with the very same warm eyes. Their
reunion was warm too. Gyuri introduced Tibor to his wife
Emi, which was short for Emilia and Tibor introduced
them both to Libby. Of course she had never seen Budapest
before so Gyuri offered to take them round town in his car.
They went to visit all the main attractions and across the
Danube to hilly Buda. It was a fantastic day.

Gyuri was a bright student and had studied hard. He
had become an engineer and worked in power plants.
Ágnes had a job in a bookshop, but now Gyuri was in a
position to help her out financially, for which she was

grateful. Consequently they were never broke and had a reasonable standard of living.

Tibor feels that he may have inspired Gyuri by the way he had left Hungary and had got on so well with his career overseas because shortly after they their reunion, Gyuri was head-hunted by a Hungarian who had emigrated to Canada. This man had offered Gyuri a job out there, which he had initially turned down. However they met again purely by chance at a party on a boat on the Danube and again he was offered the job, which this time he accepted. Gyuri and Emi emigrated to Canada and now live near Toronto.

Next day Tibor asked Libby to go and read her book that she'd brought for such a moment. He wanted to talk in greater depth to Ágnes about the family. She told Tibor that she had kept in touch with his half-sister Judit, over the years and it was with her that she had searched for him through The Red Cross. He gained the impression that it was his sister more than anyone who wanted to find him. Looking back Tibor acknowledged that due to family history he had mostly put her out of his mind as he got on with his new life in Israel and later in the UK. Ágnes asked him if he would consider meeting Judit now and Tibor said that he would think about it but would probably not see her during this visit. He said he was happy for Ágnes to tell her that she had seen him and that he was very much alive! He also asked his cousin not to give his contact details to her at this time. Ágnes told him that Judit wasn't pushy and surely would respect his wishes.

Later that day Tibor and Libby strolled down to the market at the end of Alig Street. Nothing had changed. It still looked and *smelled* the same, taking him right back to his childhood. There were the aromas of cheeses, meat and particularly the highly distinctive smell coming from the barrels of sour cabbage - Hungarian sauerkraut - which is quite distinct from its German equivalent. There were inspiring sights too like the old women in their head scarves, long dresses and aprons, who traditionally came in at dawn from the countryside every day to sell their fresh products. It was just like going to heaven for Tibor. He felt that after death he would like to be buried in one of those barrels of sauerkraut!

Those few days in Budapest were just the precursor of what was to come on subsequent visits. He had enjoyed the trip so very much, but he wouldn't have considered moving back to Hungary to make it his home again.

The family in Budapest: Ágnes' husband Tibor, Tibor, Ágnes, Gyuri and his wife Emi

Since that first visit he has gone back to Budapest nearly every year. He made one trip to the city with Jody. They went on their own without Libby. He wanted to show his son where he came from. If he went to Budapest alone he always stayed with Ágnes. She had a small spare room where she could put him up. When he went with Libby or Jody she kindly made the lounge available as well as the spare room, so they could still stay at the flat. She would not entertain for one instant the thought of them staying anywhere else other than with her.

Chapter Seventeen
Meeting Judit

On his third visit he arranged with Ágnes that he would meet his sister and she arranged that they would have lunch together at the flat. Tibor was very nervous while he waited for his sister. When the entry phone rang he did something inexplicable and unpredictable. He felt he had to do something childlike at this meeting that reflected the fact that he was her little baby brother. When Ágnes let Judit in Tibor crawled into the lounge on his hands and knees! He immediately felt he had done the wrong thing and made a fool of himself, but Judit found it very funny and his stunt went down well. He stood up and they hugged. Tibor noted she was of a 'round and cuddly' build and she was extremely warm and friendly towards him. They sat down and talked, shyly at first, but they quickly relaxed.

He thought back to the day she had turned up and stood outside the apartment when he had gone downstairs to see her and then dismissed her. He had known that his mother was angry and intuited that his father had done something wrong.

Judit

Now she was 42 and he was *not* going to reject her this time. He asked what she had been doing during the years since that first abortive meeting. She told him that she had married a man called Ferenc. They had two children - a boy István and a girl, also called Judit. Ferenc had a good job and was well paid but nonetheless he had become an alcoholic. He had decided that he wasn't able to take care of the family as he should and so one day, unexpectedly, he committed suicide by hanging himself. This had been a terrible shock and a truly severe blow to her family. Judit was left with two children to bring up and with three mouths to feed. She had an office job at that time, but after various moves around the country she ended up having to take a cleaning job in order to survive. Tibor felt strongly that their new relationship must be based on mutual affection and not on anything financial even though he had done very well in his career. Judit had formed another relationship with a married man, who already had two daughters of his own but that had not worked out because he opted to stay with his wife and children. She had a daughter by this man, called Virág, (which means flower). So now she had three children to look after.

The following day Tibor went to visit Judit and her children at home. He was warmly received as their newly-arrived uncle. Judit had previously told them everything she could about him and they were very excited to finally meet him. He could see immediately that the children were all very positive, bursting with energetic ideas and were looking forward to life. The children and their mother seemed to be very supportive of each other and were a closely functioning, healthy unit. Although Tibor and his sister could not pretend that they had grown up together, they managed to pick up many pieces and over time their relationship has grown. When he left he promised that on his return to Budapest he would definitely visit them all again. Since this time, Tibor has stayed in constant touch with all his relatives in Hungary especially since the advent of the internet, keeping contact almost daily.

Chapter Eighteen
Becoming a Captain

In 1995 Tibor was a happy co-pilot on the BAC 1-11. He had heard that the airline was thinking of introducing some Boeing 737s but thought nothing of this or how it might directly affect him, until he was walking down a corridor at work one morning and he saw one of the bosses, Captain David Ryles, coming towards him. Ryles was an intimidating man, employed by the airline to conduct the pilots' annual line checks. He would sit behind the flight crew in the cockpit and take notes on their performances, which could be both uneasy and quite unnerving. He was a cold man, who seldom smiled and he was rumoured to be the airline's hatchet man. That morning he stopped Tibor and announced that he hadn't seen Tibor's name amongst those applying for the position of Captain for the Jetstream 31, which had been advertised internally. Tibor was nearly knocked off his feet. It took just a few nanoseconds for him to realize that he was in fact being 'offered' a promotion! It might initially mean stepping backwards to fly an aircraft that he had flown almost five years earlier, nonetheless it would be a promotion because he would become a Captain and that was most certainly a forward step. Tibor had no idea that he'd been noticed or rated in any way. He'd been flying with the airline for about five years and he had the required number of flying hours under his belt to qualify him for the move from the right hand seat to the left. Tibor subsequently put in an application and was interviewed by Captain Ryles himself, who told him he would set a date to go flying with him. If that was successful he would be offered a course on the Jetstream 31 as Captain. If he passed it would be an indisputable step upwards in his career but, because he would be flying a much smaller 16-seater aircraft rather than the current 100-seater, his salary would remain the same. Tibor looked on the offer as an investment for the future. As it turned out he didn't have to do the full course because it was just under five years since he had flown the Jetstream so his type rating had not yet lapsed. He went through a short refresher course with an instructor, who was a friend of his. He had to put aside his knowledge of flying the BAC 1-11 and concentrate again on the Jetstream. He had to go out with Captain Ryles on a number of flights to get him back in tune with the aircraft. Eventually they flew with passengers, whilst line training.

On the morning he completed his final line check towards Newcastle, he was allocated a real co-pilot for the first time ever for the return journey. Ryles was sitting in the front row of the passenger seats with a long lead on his headset extending forward into the flight deck. On return to base Ryles signed him out with a final debrief. Tibor asked Ryles if he really thought he was ready. Ryles responded with, 'Well you're not going to break it are you! If you do, you'll only kill sixteen people'. He had an unusual sense of humour!

The single remaining Jetstream in the company flew only one route, from Birmingham to Newcastle and back. It made four flights a day and the crews were rostered to fly twice either in the mornings or in the afternoons. It became quite monotonous but then one day he was suddenly asked to fly to Belfast and back instead. In the context of the routine he had been flying over the past year, this added a dash of excitement, like taking a left turn towards the Irish Sea near Liverpool! The total of 14 months on the Jetstream came to an end when....

Chapter Nineteen
The Boeing 737

The airline had leased several Boeing 737s and again Tibor strangely had another corridor encounter, but this time with Captain Chris Ward. Young Chris had risen quickly through the ranks at the airline and was now the boss of the 737 fleet. Tibor had always assumed due to his 4.5 years on the BAC1-11 that he might eventually be offered a position in the left hand seat of that aircraft, as Captain. But no, this wasn't the case.

BA/Maersk Air Ltd Boeing 737

He was offered a Captain's seat on the 737 fleet! He was absolutely delighted but found it hard to believe that they thought so well of him. He was then put on a Boeing

737 course. It was now 1996, the end of his sixth year in this company.

Tibor had never been near the cockpit of a 737 so to go into the Captain's position straight off was really quite something! He felt that if he could crack this one he could do anything in aviation.

Tibor and three other pilots were sent up to Coalville in the East Midlands. British Midland Airways ran the course for Maersk Air. The company had a full facility: the simulator and the ground staff to teach everything about the 737. The course lasted for several weeks and the four pilots were accommodated in a very good hotel called The Priest House.

Often Tibor found these training courses tedious but this particular course was incredibly good and the airplane made so much sense to him. He felt destined to fly it as if it was made for him! It threw him back to the day when Shraga had arranged for him to sit in the 707 cockpit. The 737 and the 707 cockpits are almost identical. In point of fact the 707 had four engines whereas the 737 had just two. The 707 also had a flight engineer with his own panels and seating behind the pilots, which the 737 didn't need as it had a crew of just two pilots. As far as Tibor was concerned this was truly the realization of a dream and he slowly developed a love for this airplane. It almost compared to drumming with Led Zeppelin – being in John Bonham's place on stage.

He passed all the written exams just as he always did. Then he was paired up with a Co-pilot, Andy, throughout the simulator course which needed hard work and long hours each evening. They practiced the various standard operating procedures and memory drills using a cardboard 'cockpit' that his partner had created for the purpose on his own initiative. Tibor bought him a couple of beers for this!

Having eventually passed the whole course, it was time to fly the real thing. How exciting it was to walk out onto the apron in Birmingham on a wet Saturday morning with that beautiful 737 awaiting its three crew to bring it to life.

He and Andy, plus Nigel the trainer, prepared to fly it up to Prestwick from Birmingham to do circuit practice for the day. Tibor remembers being the first to handle the aircraft. Having started the engines and slowly taxied it to the runway, he performed his first take off in it with the trainer sitting in the right hand seat. It felt big and very powerful, especially as it had an empty cabin for the day.

This was *the* moment Tibor had dreamt of for decades and worked extremely hard to achieve. The high-pitched whistle and the dull roar of the engines, controlled by his fists at 27000 rpm each was celestial music to his ears. He was 'Skygod'!

On route, navigating the flight with its sophisticated Flight Management Computer was easier to handle than any other aircraft to date. The cockpit was very much designed with pilots in mind! Arriving at Prestwick, they joined into the local circuit and Tibor began preparations for his first landing. Controlling the real 737 felt easier than in the simulator, it was much less twitchy and it felt bigger and more stable than previous aircraft he had handled. After the first touch-down Nigel took over and performed a rolling take off. This means converting a landing into another take-off by re-applying power and retracting the landing flaps to take off position. This was a manoeuvre purely reserved for trainers. After a few circuits Nigel was happy and they played musical chairs. Nigel sat in the left hand seat, Andy in the right and Tibor sat behind them on the jump seat. It was now Andy's turn to feel the beast.

At the end of that day and back at Birmingham they were both signed out and cleared for line training! This meant that next he would be flying with another Training Captain who would be sitting in the right hand seat and with a cabin full of fare-paying passengers. This final stage of training took approximately a month, culminating in a final check.

Somewhere at 37,000 feet

The very next flight he was in full control of the aircraft and crew as Captain. It took a little while for this to finally sink in but it was true. He was no longer in charge of a Jetstream 31 with just 16 passengers on board but was now flying an aircraft with 150 people sitting behind him, sometimes for as many as four flights a day. This he felt was what his life was meant to be about.

Chapter Twenty
In and Out of Ryanair

Over these years he visited Hungary frequently sometimes alone, sometimes with Libby and sometimes with Jody. He recalls once flying from Heathrow with the Hungarian airline, Malév, in a very old Russian Tupolev 154. This aircraft had three engines and had anhedral wings, which point downwards from the fuselage. Aircraft like the 737 had dihedral wings, which point upwards. The anhedral design was adopted by the Russians to make their aircraft look distinctively different to Western airplanes. Halfway through the flight he showed the stewardess his licence and told her he was Hungarian and worked as flight crew in the UK. He asked if the Captain would mind if he went up onto the flight deck for a chat. She came back and told him that the Captain would like to meet him.

When he went in he was surprised to find that there were three men in there until he remembered that the Tupolev was very old and required a flight engineer. He recalls that the Captain was a very nice guy and they chatted amiably about their work and conditions. The conversation eventually came round to comparing salaries and Tibor was amazed when the Captain told him that he earned just £300 a month. Tibor asked him why he did such a demanding job for so little and the Captain responded, 'Because we're stupid!' They discussed the Tupolev's performance capabilities and he was told by the Captain that it was so grossly overpowered that he could put the aircraft on its tail and it would still carry on climbing! He asked Tibor if he would like to remain on the flight deck for the landing as they had a spare jump-seat. So Tibor stayed there for the rest of the flight and was amazed at the vast differences in the techniques they employed for landing the aircraft.

Before he became a pilot he had always made a point of trying to visit flight decks when he was a passenger, sometimes taking Jody in with him. Later Jody joined Tibor on his own flight deck on some of his trips. As a child of a pilot there are some privileges that come with the territory and going on trips on a flight deck with your father was a particularly special one. Sadly Jody's generation may well have been one of the last ones to be able to enjoy this experience.

Before 9/11 the flight deck doors were seldom locked, but after that everything changed. Those doors are now always locked on every flight. The consequences of 9/11 on the airline industry were absolutely devastating. People stopped travelling and all the airlines started cutting back and security checks were cranked up. The effect was startling on Tibor's airline too. Over 2002 the operation was scaled right back. The airline started to return its 737s to the lessors one by one, taking on smaller jets with 30, 40 and 50-seater capacities, called the CRJ, Canadian Regional Jet. He was scheduled to go on a type rating course for one of these. Transferring to this type would have been a considerable backwards step in his career. He told Libby he wasn't interested in this regression – going from captaining a 737 to a CRJ was not something he could tolerate. He decided that after 12 years with the airline he would have to leave the company.

He started to talk with other airlines and in particular with Ryanair, which unlike others was growing dynamically and expanding fast. They claimed they were the cheapest in the industry and with a Boeing contract they were taking weekly deliveries of brand new 737 aircraft, which went straight on line in Ryanair colours. They were setting up bases all over Europe as fast as they could in cities like Frankfurt and Milan. This was engineered under the aggressive leadership of Michael O'Leary. Although Tibor really didn't like his style he was impressed by the man's forthright approach and by his cheeky confidence. He *nearly* took his hat off to him.

Tibor applied to the company and he was accepted as a Captain on the New Generation of the 737, which was somewhat different to the version he was used to. There were winglets at the end of the wings and the flight deck had been radically brought forward into the computer age. Gone were some of the old dials, now in their place were five big TV screens. He received his welcoming letter to Ryanair as a 737 Captain, informing him that he would be notified of his start date and base in due course. He immediately resigned from Maersk Air with a very good payoff because the company was looking for staff who would take voluntary redundancy. His pension was not going to be all that good because he had been suspicious about any pension system since the Maxwell Affair and so had kept his contributions to a minimum. Using this payoff, he and Libby chose to put a deposit on a flat in the London Docklands, seeing this as being a possible alternative to a pension for them in years to come. Once the flat was built, with the help of a local agent they were able to let it out straight away. They were in fact looking for capital growth for the long term more than rental income.

It was then a question of waiting for that call from Ryanair to be given a start date for his course and his operations base. His preference for a base was Stansted for various reasons. This was by far the biggest Ryanair base in the UK, with some 46 aircraft. When the call finally came in January 2003 he was informed of a start date and that his base would be Frankfurt Hahn Airport. He acknowledged the start date and thanked them, then turned to Libby and said, 'This isn't going to happen. It's just not going to happen.'

Despite this they thought they should at least check the location out and see if they could entertain the thought of him operating out of Frankfurt. They bought two return tickets with Ryanair from Stansted to Frankfurt for £1.65 each(!) online. They found that the Moselle Valley area was really pleasant with the river and the vineyards, but they spoke no German and could not find any estate agents when they went to enquire about possible properties to rent. The only places they encountered English speakers were in the pubs and taverns! This wasn't going to get them anywhere. Tibor began to wonder if he was going to have to live there on his own with his family left behind in England. It was not a happy prospect but with no other job offers on his horizon he accepted the start date. He decided that from the moment he started he would use every means at his disposal to attempt to change the base, going as far up the chain of command as he was able.

The course began in January 2003 and he spent his first week in East Midlands Airport in a classroom with 25 other pilots. Every spare minute he had he used to try and convince Ryanair to change his allotted operating base. As part of the induction course the class was taken to their main Operations Headquarters at Stansted. He could not accept that given their high turn-over rate with pilots and with the amount of aircraft based at Stansted, they could not find a position for him. The ideal plan was to sell their house in the Midlands and rent one in Cambridge while they looked for some land they could develop from the proceeds of the sale. Together with a builder from Libby's family, after the project's completion they would sell on the development at a profit. They would then keep repeating the process for years to come. They were hoping to slowly grow their finances this way, while Tibor worked for a good salary with Ryanair. But it wasn't to be.

During his second week on the course he caught sight of Declan Dooney, the very man who had recruited him into Ryanair. He told Declan that he had a serious problem with being based at Frankfurt and that he could see that it wasn't going to work out. Declan appreciated that there was 'indeed a real problem' and said he would make some phone calls to see if he could work something out. Tibor began to feel optimistic, but his hopes were soon dashed when Declan returned and informed him that nothing could be done about reassigning him to a different base at this time. So that was that. He downed tools and walked out. It was a slap in the face and it took him back to his deeply disappointing attempts to break into the music business. There was a difference this time though because *he* had made the decision to walk out. This time his pride was not badly dented by the experience. He told Libby that he felt he had done everything he could do in aviation and after these 12 years he felt it might be time to stop flying.

They agreed that they had enough money to take their time while they thought about how they might get involved fully in the property business. It was a huge relief to be free of the constant grinding of medicals, line and simulator checks. The latter could be a harrowing experience given that it was always possible to fail. Each simulator check required three to four days of preparation and they happened every six months and each check was different. It was impossible to prepare for every eventuality. If a pilot failed the first check he was given a second chance but if he failed again, well, that could have been that!

He cast around for something to involve himself in and they decided that they would apply for planning permission to build a small house at the bottom of their garden for profit.

Chapter Twenty One
bmibaby

They waited to hear about their planning application but eventually they were turned down. They appealed using a specialist in this field but their plans were again rejected. This was disappointing and frustrating.

Then right out of the blue Tibor had a phone call from one of his old flying mates at Maersk Air called Paul Kelley. Paul asked what he had been up to lately and he told him about their development plans being turned down by Stratford District Council and that he wasn't doing much else at the time. Paul asked if Tibor had heard about a new airline called bmibaby which had just taken 20 pilots from Maersk Air, which incidentally closed down about a year after Tibor had left. Paul inquired if he had thought of applying to them for a job. Tibor said that he'd heard of the airline but that he wasn't interested. Paul told him that bmibaby were on the lookout for more 737-rated pilots. Tibor wasn't going to take this further, but Paul said take the number anyway, in case! Having put the phone down immediately and almost on auto-pilot he picked up the phone and dialed the number. The phone was answered by Ian Laurie, the Captain, in charge of recruitment. Tibor told him that he was part of the same 737 team from which he had just recruited 20 pilots and was wondering if there were any remaining vacancies. Ian was interested and asked Tibor to send in his paperwork and CV and that he would get back to him. At that moment *everything* changed again! He was suddenly feeling very excited about the chance of flying once more. Tibor realized that walking out of Ryanair earlier in the year clearly hadn't quite placed the dot at the end of the sentence. The embers of aviation it seems were not fully extinguished just yet.

Tibor was certain that he would hear back from Ian but after two weeks of patient waiting he picked up the phone again. This time frustratingly he had to leave a message. Another few days went by but still no response came. Out of sheer annoyance and total loss of patience one morning straight after breakfast he grabbed the phone to make contact. To his relief Ian answered and, when Tibor asked what had happened to his application, the response came as music to his ears. Ian said 'I was going to call you today anyway' and added that he wanted to meet for a chat.

Tibor always sported a close-cropped beard but Libby

suggested that he might consider shaving for the interview. He thought about this for a moment and chose not to. His interview was to be held at Donnington Hall, the impressive stately home-like headquarters of BMI, which was owned by Michael Bishop – a famous name in aviation. BMI was previously known as British Midland Airways.

He arrived at reception for the meeting and as Ian turned up Tibor was delighted to see that they *both* had exactly the same type of cropped beard! Soul brothers! Often an airline interview involves three people, like a panel of judges where one is friendly, the second is hostile and the third one is neutral. This interview was conducted by Ian on his own. He needed to see whether, in his opinion Tibor would get along well with the crews and this was one of Tibor's strong cards. That and of course being able to fly an airplane! Within minutes he was hired and was told that his base would be Manchester. Tibor's response was, 'Well, Ian, that's a lot closer than Frankfurt-Hahn!'

However, a few weeks before starting in Manchester Tibor heard from a colleague Mark, who had decided not to take up his own position in Cardiff which was due to start shortly. It was suggested that perhaps Tibor could ask bmibaby if *he* could have Mark's vacant place in Cardiff instead of Manchester. On the day when Mark had planned to inform bmibaby about this he called Tibor first, as arranged. Then allowing a few minutes for Mark's call to take effect Tibor called the airline, saying that he knew of an emerging position in Cardiff, which he would prefer to that of Manchester. Here is how he got his way – that call was taken by a young lady in personnel called Rachel. During part of the conversation Tibor mentioned his past life in Israel. Her voice immediately brightened and she said to him that she too had spent time there in a Kibbutz when she was younger and loved every minute of it. This connection eventually saved him from hours on end commuting up and down the M6.

Rachel suggested that Tibor would arrange to pick up his flying manuals from Donnington Hall on a day when she too was scheduled to be there, as normally she was based in London. She contrived to then set up a 'chance' meeting with Captain John Robertson, the bmibaby Operations Director, who would be in a position to approve of a base change. The plan came together in the car park out of all places when she spotted John walking towards his car. She introduced the two of them saying to John, 'Tibor is one of our new captains and he has a request of a change of base'. John agreed and replied that as long as there was a position available in Cardiff, he would have no objection to the swap and that she could action this.

That was the green light for Tibor and Libby to travel to South Wales to look around for a house to rent. They saw a lot of unsuitable properties and were becoming utterly disheartened, by the time they walked into the last estate agency at closing time. They had a detached cottage available that apparently 'nobody liked' and it was so late in the day that no one would be available to show them around. Nevertheless, Libby and Tibor drove to the next village to see it from the outside anyway. The moment they spotted it they knew it *had* to be the one! Peeking through the windows, looking at the garden and considering the negligible amount of rent, their minds were made up for them. They drove the two hour journey home that night feeling that, after all, the day had been a resounding success and couldn't wait to call the agent the next morning. Soon the contract was signed for 12 months.

It was mutually decided that at the age of 23 Jody could remain at the family home. His brief included looking after the three cats, numerous plants and at least the structure of the house if not its décor!

Any time Tibor had two days off they would race back home to the Midlands. They'd leave after his last flight had landed, which meant heading for home at about one or two in the morning, returning to Cardiff after a day at home in time for Tibor to make the routine early start after a late finish. Early starts always followed a late finish around days off. They did this for a year and during that time they had both learned to love Cardiff and being near the sea. In the second year they managed to let out their home to a family for a very good rent.

By then Jody had just opened a menswear shop in Leamington Spa and they arranged local accommodation for him there. It was 2004 and now, with hardly any commuting, they were able to settle down more and enjoy their free time better. They spent a lot of it exploring the South Glamorgan coast with its beautiful beaches, cliffs, walks, forests and the sea!

SelMate

During this time they met a very lovely couple called Jenny and John, who both originated from the Midlands. Jenny had recently moved to the area to live with John. A mutual friend, Nigel, called Libby to say that she might like to meet with her as she was new to the locality. During their first pub meeting John and Tibor got talking. John was fascinated that Tibor was an Airline Pilot not least because he had a Private Pilot's Licence too. So they talked a lot about aviation that evening.

Tibor was equally intrigued by John's occupation. He was MD of Roland in the UK, the mighty Japanese electronic musical instrument company, which was based in Swansea. For a while Tibor had been toying with the idea of buying one of their kits. So John's appearance in Tibor's life was another miracle! He mentioned that he had seen a Roland kit demonstration once at the NEC by a young, bright and brilliantly talented drummer, who gave explanations about the kit through a Madonna-type headset. The kit was amazing. The sound was better than any acoustic kit he'd ever played. After the demo he had a few questions for the young drummer. He was very helpful. John responded with, 'Oh yes, that'll be our Ben!' He meant Ben Stone, who was the Chief Roland Demonstrator. Tibor asked John if, as MD of the company, he could arrange a new kit with a bit of a discount. John's response was, 'Of course I can, how's about a 40% staff discount?' Tibor bought him another pint! John added, 'You know what, I'll ask Ben to deliver the kit to you in person and spend the whole day with you to help you set it up.' Tibor needed a drink!

In the event things didn't turn out exactly like that. The kit arrived a week earlier than planned. Tibor unpacked it and set it up as best he could. It worked, but he knew that when Ben came it would be just perfect. Ben arrived one morning at about 10am. Libby was out but Tibor immediately recognised him from the demo day. Ben of course didn't remotely remember their conversation. They spent the day together and he was an absolute star. They went for lunch, talked and played drums all day! It was amazing. They became friends and have kept in touch ever since.

This kit has enabled Tibor to play even as early as four in the morning because with headphones you play to yourself. From the outside it sounds a bit like someone tapping a piece of soft plastic with some sticks! It's very quiet though in the headphones it's like being in a huge cave with the biggest, most thunderous sounding drum kit in the world! He could play along to different bands and also could easily record himself on top. When Tibor gave Ben a CD of some of these recordings he responded with, 'You are the most accurate and precise guy I've ever known playing to someone else's music'. Nice compliment thought Tibor. These days Ben is Tom Jones' drummer. He also plays with Mike and the Mechanics.

A little while later his old London mate Selwyn (now living in South Africa) and Tibor 'found' each other on the internet again. They realised that, although they were separated by two continents, they could now start making music again together for fun online. Tibor's kit provided them with that facility. Had he been still playing acoustic drums this would not have been possible without hiring a recording studio at a huge expense. The project SelMate was born. SelMate is SELwyn and his MATE, Tibor! The concept was truly amazing. Selwyn was writing really exciting, sometimes heavy and complicated tunes, playing all the instruments himself, to which he attached a 'guide' drum track. He would then email this to Tibor who would work on the song and come up with his own versions and parts. Selwyn also sent him the same track clean, without any guide and with just the count-in at the beginning. Tibor had the luxury that all the tracks were in perfect time

227

already as Selwyn recorded them, so he didn't need a click track. He just had to play along with the existing timing, recording onto the clean track. It sounded incredible. He could record a song in many parts using a clever piece of software called Cubase, which meant he didn't have to play all the track from start to finish and which made life easier. Selwyn would then convert Tibor's MiDi 'signals' into proper sounds in his home studio in Cape Town. The mixes that he returned sounded like they had spent thousands of pounds in studios!

They asked Storm to create a logo, which gave them a visual identity. Storm created an amazing picture **all** for free! This is the guy that charges Pink Floyd and Led Zeppelin, but not SelMate!

SelMate is currently having a break, but, since it's all just for fun, it doesn't really matter. These tracks can all be heard on the internet by anyone who's interested.

All Change

Then out of the blue bmibaby announced that they were opening a new base in... Birmingham! Tibor and Libby had just signed the contract with their tenants and were predictably dismayed by the timing of events. Fortunately however this new base would take months to set up, giving the tenancy time to run for its full year.

He called Chris Ward, who was now part of the bmibaby management team and who had been instrumental in transferring Tibor originally onto the 737 at Maersk and asked him what his chances were of being transferred to Birmingham, given that he was already on a transfer request list for East Midlands. Their intention was always to return to the Midlands when possible. Chris confirmed that this could and would be done in due course. Their tenants were not too unhappy about moving out after their year's contract had run its course and moved to a house in a nearby village. In the summer of 2005 Tibor and Libby moved back into their home and Jody stayed in his accommodation in Leamington Spa. Everything was back to how it had been.

Pilot Perks

Having settled back into Birmingham Tibor found that he very much enjoyed the base, his colleagues and the routes he was flying.

The airline used to carry out the servicing of their aircraft in different locations and countries. One of these turned out to be Lufthansa Technic in Budapest! When Tibor caught wind of this he kept asking the Chief Pilot, Pete Durnford, whether he could be scheduled for one of these positioning flights when the aircraft was flown empty - ferried - to Budapest for maintenance or for the return journey. In either case - on the return or the outbound flight - the crew would fly as passengers on another airline to get there or home. One day he was called out from an 11am standby to do one of these pick up flights. He was delirious with excitement unlike on the other occasions when he'd been called out from standby.

Tibor and his First Officer flew out that afternoon with Ryanair from East Midlands airport to Budapest. They were met in the terminal by two people from the hangar. One of them, who appeared to be the boss, called Zoli started talking to them in really good English and Tibor responded in Hungarian! Zoli was staggered. He didn't expect a Hungarian response. They were well used to dealing with the British crews as they came and went, but this was different for them. This was exciting!

So, instead of heading towards the hangar, Zoli said, 'Come on upstairs I want to buy us all a coffee'. They sat down to talk and Zoli asked a lot of questions about Tibor and appeared genuinely interested in how he came to be an airline pilot in England. They sat for a while and became friends immediately.

Zoli was one of the managers at the Lufthansa hangar and he was tasked with completing the paperwork before they took the serviced, empty aircraft back into the sky, home-bound. Empty meant that there were *no* seats even in the passenger cabin. These had been left behind at East Midlands Airport in the hangar so that the Hungarians could take up the cabin floor more easily for access to the systems.

Before departure they were given a gift pack, like all crews, containing a famous Hungarian bottle of Tokai and some interesting information about Hungary and its amazing culinary background. This was indeed a very special touch on Tibor's very special day out.

They took off from exactly the same airport he had flown from with his mother in 1967 at the age of 12. This was now *his turn*. He had grown up! Flying over the beautifully lit up city for the first time as a pilot was a most memorable experience. He quietly fought back a few tears.

In October 2009 the company gave him another 'gift'. He was to fly an empty aircraft into Budapest. This time he was given more notice so he was able to arrange to stay in Budapest for three days before catching his pre-arranged return flight with Ryanair. He informed all his relatives that he would be coming. They were all very excited when he announced, 'On this occasion I will be flying myself in!' After a very early start they took off from East Midlands with a most special and surprising call sign for the flight (the letters and numbers used to communicate with Air Traffic Control). This was '*Baby 72 Tango Juliet*', where TJ were Tibor's initials. This had been arranged sneakily behind his back by bmibaby's operations department.

Passenger Perks

Before 9/11 visits to flight decks were allowed with the approval of the Captain. These would normally take place in the cruise when the crew was less busy. Indeed Tibor had made many such, enjoyable eye-opening visits to flight decks before he became an airline pilot. Often one of the cabin crew would call on the inter-phone, or come and see them with a coffee and say, 'There's a passenger with a child, who would like a visit'. Whenever the conditions were right they were able to accommodate these requests. But when they turned up with a two year old child it became obvious that it was the parent that wanted the visit - not the two year old, who actually spent the whole time trying to get out! The crew didn't really mind. The older children or the adults often asked questions about the systems with questions like, 'Where are we?' Tibor normally let his First Officer deal with these questions. Sometimes passengers wanted a visit more for reasons of reassurance than interest. These were the 'Frightened to Fly' types and they were mostly female and of any age. They were sometimes on their first ever flight. When one of these people was allowed in Tibor used to ask the questions. Inevitably they would tell him how nervous they felt and that it might have taken them weeks to work up to this day! Tibor then proceeded to try to make them feel more comfortable and reassured and often added at the end, 'Look we may actually have something in common today as this is *my* first day on this aircraft type and I feel quite nervous'! This would normally to do the trick and was followed by a nervous laugh and a hasty exit!

Chapter Twenty Two
The Two Reunions

In August 2010, some 32 years after their last gig in Israel Beber the singer, decided that the band Bereshit should get back together on stage one last time in their original line-up. Tibor flew to Israel a couple of days before the historic gig, having arranged leave with the airline months in advance. In the preceding three decades Tibor had had very little contact with the rest of the band. Beber was on Facebook so they had been in touch occasionally. Benjo, the bass player had no internet presence! Shimon their lead guitarist had disappeared for at least 25 years. No one knew where he was or whether he was alive or dead. In the last five years there had been reports of sightings of him around Tel Aviv and later on in Haifa. The rumours were that he had no teeth left and was mentally vacant! He looked like a vagrant and had no family or friends. This was a big shock to Tibor as they had spent so many years playing together, but in a way it was predictable. He had always been heavily into drugs and although they had that LSD night together, Tibor has given that drug a wide berth after that! Shimon on the other hand, went on and on taking drugs until he'd effectively become a zombie. Tibor found this so unbearable that he decided never to seek him out.

During his last two visits to Israel he'd met up with Beber just to reminisce about the good old days. Beber had always remained a singer and had been known to build up and then desert quite a few bands. He'd had some local success with one or two versions of a Pink Floyd tribute band. Tibor had seen them and thought he was truly magnificent. He had certainly kept his voice in good order.

Benjo had become a household name playing bass with his band Benzin. They'd had numerous hits and played many stadium-size gigs. It seemed that finally, after all these years, he had found his calling. But it was not to be for long. Benzin's singer and main persona, Yehuda Poliker, quit the band to follow a solo career and had become one of the most successful artists in recent years in Israel.

When Beber asked him if he would consider doing a one-off gig with the band Tibor's first question was about Shimon. Beber said he'd had contact with him and that surprisingly he was keen to do it. Throughout his time 'in orbit' Shimon, had kept up his guitar playing, turning up in a variety of places and taking to the stage with different people. He had even made a recording with Peter Green of Fleetwood Mac fame. Although he had his treasured Gibson Les Paul stolen, which broke his heart, he remained unstoppable as far as his music was concerned. Tibor tried to imagine what it would be like meeting him again after three decades. And that meeting was very different from what he had expected.

When Tibor arrived at Ben Gurion airport he was picked up by an old friend called Rani. They had kept in touch and he had visited Tibor in England more than once. He had three children and a lovely wife called Nili. Rani's parents were also Hungarian so as Tibor puts it, 'he had to be a great guy!' He spent the first night at their house before setting off to Haifa with Rani the next day. They were going to a reunion party in a café in Haifa with many old friends, who neither of them had seen for decades. It was an exciting prospect.

As they were ascending the steep road towards the café on Mount Carmel there he was walking up towards the top. Tibor could hardly believe his eyes. Shimon! Tibor asked Rani to stop the car. He got out, called his name and went up to him. Shimon turned to Tibor and obviously didn't recognise him. Tibor asked in Hebrew, 'Shimon, do you have any idea who I am?' He looked back blankly and Tibor said, 'Look, it's me, Tibor.' This produced an enormous grin, which did reveal badly decaying teeth. He looked dishevelled with long, unkempt hair. They embraced and Tibor was pleasantly surprised to find him in relatively good shape. Tibor pointed to Rani, who Shimon recognised, and then they told him about the reunion party. He asked Shimon if he would like to join them. He said he would but that he had no money. Tibor brushed away that problem and he got into the car. They talked briefly and Shimon said that he'd heard that Tibor had become an airline pilot, which had impressed him.

They arrived at the café and there were many people there, some of whom he recognized immediately, others it took longer to remember. Most of them knew Shimon and were completely amazed to see them turn up together, not having seen Tibor or Shimon for 35 years. Tibor reminded Shimon that they had a rehearsal scheduled for that night. He said he'd be there and Tibor was amazed, as he'd expected some signs of madness, but at that stage he saw none. Tibor found it difficult to concentrate with any one individual and to have a conversation because there was always someone else he recognised and wanted to speak to. The party continued until it was time to head on towards the Bay of Haifa. Shimon had already left, promising to catch up at the rehearsals later. Beber was going to pick him up and drive him to the venue.

Tibor was staying with another old Israeli friend called Avi, whose mother lived out in Haifa bay. Avi was now living in London and had remained friends with Tibor ever since school age. Avi had made this journey too for the gig, the reunion of friends in the cafe and also to visit his mother. Avi had two beautiful daughters and a crazy Irish wife, Thelma in England. Avi's mother welcomed Tibor. She remembered him from his younger days.

That time in Israel was particularly hot and even the locals were talking about it. They were used to the heat of course, but in the day it was well over 40 degrees and without air-conditioning life was impossible. There are times when the temperature reaches 50 degrees in Israel. Those spells are called the Hamsin, which means 50 in Arabic. When he was a school-boy and there was a Hamsin they were sent home. No one could study in that kind of heat!

That evening Tibor went to a school basement for the band's reunion rehearsal. There was another band playing at the time, but his mates were already there. They caught up with each other and they were invited to use the other band's equipment to begin preparing the two songs they had decided to attempt. They had chosen to play material from the old days when they were kids as their audience would be around the same age and would know the songs, which were written by Grand Funk Railroad. It was absolutely pure rock and nothing at all to do with funk! The drums that Tibor had been given for the rehearsal were far from adequate. He hadn't even brought his own sticks with him as he'd been told that everything would be there for him but he wasn't happy. This was no time to throw a tantrum, or to walk out! He had to make do.

When they started the first song they immediately ran into sound issues. There were quite a few people watching them, including some friends from earlier in the day at the reunion in the café. Tibor didn't think this was a great idea as they really needed time to re-adjust to each other. The band had just one hour to get their ideas and the sound sorted. Then, unhappy as they were, they had to vacate the space to allow the band whose equipment they were using to get on with their rehearsal. It only dawned on Tibor then, that this band would also be playing the next evening at the gig. They parted company to meet again the next day at the venue. Tibor felt far from confident. He knew that there would be a lot of people watching them and he badly wanted them to sound good and together!

Sleeping was incredibly uncomfortable even though the air-con was on all night He didn't have it in his bedroom so he'd placed a fan just inches from his head. It was far from satisfactory. Being Hungarian and European, he really missed the British weather that night! Next day they were joined by a couple of friends and went to do some sightseeing in Akko, which is not far from Haifa Bay. It is a mixed city, 72 percent Jewish and 28 percent Arab. Despite all the media frenzy Israelis and Arabs can co-exist in harmony.

They went to the market in Akko and had lunch in a most unlikely looking Arab restaurant called Said's. It appeared to be like a factory canteen with fluorescent strip lights and revolving fans on the ceiling. The queue outside indicated that this place was worth the wait, even though it meant getting cooked himself in the heat! After half an hour they got a table for four and welcomed the air-con's benefit. The menu was not extensive, but they were all starving. They were served hummus, which Tibor loves, with fresh salads, gherkins and other sours and hot pitta bread. The hummus was served in a deep soup plate with the finest of oil drizzled into the middle with the freshest of parsley. It was the most famous Arab hummus restaurant in Israel and for good reason. They had cold beer. When they'd finished and paid the very modest bill they staggered out into the heat.

Tibor arrived at the venue in the late afternoon for the evening's gig. It was large enough to hold 300 people with tables. To his relief there was a drum kit already on the stage and it was far superior to the kit he'd had at the rehearsal. The heat was grinding and any movement produced a bucket of sweat from a squeezed T-shirt. Drumming was certainly not going to cool him down! He snatched an electric fan and fixed it on the kit. They did a sound check mostly for the benefit of a sound man, who was going to do the mixing for all the acts. After that they left for a few hours.

Avi and Tibor were invited to an old friend Rachel's beautiful house for dinner. She was a good friend from the old days and now like them she had grown-up children.

She had prepared a lot of different Mediterranean dishes and Tibor eat modestly still full from the lunchtime hummus. There were quite a few friends present and there was a great atmosphere.

When they arrived at the venue there was already a large crowd and Tibor immediately started recognising people he hadn't seen in decades. There were other musicians there too and they shared catch-up stories. Some of them had heard about his job and just couldn't put the young and the older Tibor together! Then all his friends from the reunion café afternoon arrived - some 20 or 30 of them. The circulating went on until the place was full and the first band came on. There were about eight acts on that night and Tibor's band were to be the highlight of the evening, which made him nervous. A lot of the other acts were much more together than they were going to be. But without enough rehearsal time they couldn't hope for brilliance. This was to be no Pink Floyd reunion!

At this point there was no sign of Shimon. Beber was half expecting him not to turn up at all and wondered if he'd be in a fit state to play if he did. Tibor tried not to think about it. They expected to go on at about 10 o'clock and at about a quarter to ten Shimon walked through the door and everyone started cheering. Tibor was very relieved.

When their turn came they climbed on stage and got busy setting up for a few minutes. Beber had organized the evening and was introducing the acts too. When they were ready he introduced the band, mentioning their names. The audience was genuinely excited to see the four of them together again. They got going with the first number *Are you Ready?* which had often been their show opener. It was an easy song to play and quite up-tempo. They followed with *I'm your Captain*, which obviously had a deep resonance for Tibor! So, that was it. Two numbers and 10 minutes later they were off the stage. They could have done an encore had they had more material prepared. The audience wanted more, but they couldn't deliver. Tibor was more than happy to have got through those two numbers without a disaster! Beber went back on stage after them with the current band he was in, but Tibor just stood outside as the audience left saying his goodbyes and feeling great. On reflection Tibor felt it was well worth travelling all that way to resurrect the old flame just once more. This was their last ever gig.

Chapter Twenty Three
Richard January - RIP

In the summer of 2010 two friends had come to visit Libby and Tibor at their house and were expecting to stay the night. They had arrived in the late afternoon and they were all sitting in the garden enjoying a bottle of fine red wine. Then unexpectedly there came a phone call from Suzy, Libby's younger sister in Cambridge. Tibor took the call. She sounded very disturbed.

Tibor thought that Suzy would be ringing to tell them that their mother, Winifred, had died as she was approaching 100 and was very frail. They had been expecting this call to come at some point. But what she had to tell them came as an enormous shock. Richard, Libby's brother, had died suddenly and unexpectedly that day. Shaken by the news Tibor passed the phone over to Libby. Then he informed the guests, who could already see that something was very wrong. Without a moment's hesitation they stood up and said they had decided to go home as this was clearly no time for entertainment.

As Libby came off the phone stunned, they said their goodbyes to the guests. Then they just looked at each other in total disbelief.

Richard, Tibor, Peter Eastwood, Libby and Anne Gardener

Richard was just 68. In today's terms he was far from old. He had been a farmer all his life and suffered from late onset Diabetes Type II, which had been kept under control for many years by diet and medication. The condition had recently moved on to Type I. He then had daily injections of Insulin. As far as the family was concerned the situation was under control and he was expected to live a long and fruitful life.

Libby felt she needed to be with her sisters and mother as soon as possible. She and her two sisters decided not to tell their mother immediately fearing it would be too much of a shock for her. The next day they all got together with her doctor on standby in the adjacent room and very gently broke this very sad news to her. She took the death of her only son incredibly calmly and understood exactly what had happened. Apart from the weakness of her short-term memory she was physically fine and mentally alert. However the burden of this grief slowly took its toll. About a year after Richard's death she moved into a care home as she was gradually needing increasing amount of care. She celebrated her 100th birthday with her three daughters: Libby, Suzy, Rose - Libby's twin, and Anne, Richard's long-term partner and some of her grandchildren. She received her telegram from The Queen much to her delight. Sadly Tibor was at work that day and couldn't attend.

At the beginning of 2011 Libby had a letter from the family solicitors. It came as a bolt of lightning out of a sunny sky! It informed them that Libby and her sisters were to receive a very large amount of money each from Richard's estate. He never had children and it turned out that he was quite wealthy. Anne was to receive half of everything and the girls a sixth each. For Libby and Tibor this amounted to a life changing sum of money. Richard had been a most charming, kind, witty and humorous man, who had always been very warm towards Tibor and had taken a particular interest in his career. He had known Tibor since he was just 24 as the drummer with his long hair and torn jeans. He may not have appeared to be the type of person who would eventually become a captain of a 737, but right from the beginning Richard had always warmly welcomed him as part of the family. None of his sisters or his in-laws ever imagined just how wealthy Richard would turn out to be and never considered that any of them might become beneficiaries of anything he left behind, or indeed that he would even die!

Before this letter arrived Tibor was already working on a 75% flying roster due to his insistent desire to reach the age of 60 and to retire in relatively good health. He himself had been diagnosed with Diabetes Type II in 2009. His job required that he had an annual medical check, which meant that his diabetic condition must have been less than a year old. He immediately took steps to try and arrest any further deterioration and started cycling every day. He cut out all alcohol and went to a nutritionist for advice on losing weight. This all worked wonderfully fast for him. He had to stop flying temporarily due to the regulations concerning the taking of medication. However after a month and a half his doctor told him that he had 'practically cured himself' and all his blood tests since then have been negative. He's been able to drink alcohol and eat some sweets without them having any effect on his glucose levels. He continues to have blood tests four times a year out of choice.

After three months he returned to work in the spring of 2009 but only on a 50% roster. This rhythm was good and not too taxing. Following the solicitor's letter in early 2011 he had a discussion with Libby and decided to go for early retirement and gave the company three months' notice. On the 9th of August 2011 he was to command his last flight, to Amsterdam and back.

By prior arrangement with Birmingham Air Traffic Control Tibor was able to fly right over his house on the way home at a slow speed. Jody recorded the event on video from the garden.

Tibor's actual last landing

Afterwards on that warm August evening a wonderful retirement party with friends and some family was arranged for him. Libby had bought him a pair of white feathered, angelic looking wings which he had to wear and ritually *hang up* at the end of the party!

Tibor's water cannon salute

On this day he had completed the sum total of 13,000 flying hours, equating to approximately 1.5 years living in the sky.

Eventually the time came when he and Libby sat down to discuss the future. The discussion included, amongst other things, what should be done with her inheritance as they both wished to include Jody and Bill in their hugely improved circumstances. Tibor also hoped to include his Hungarian family. Any gifts in their direction could have a significant effect on their lives. It was a real chance to make a difference and they did just that. They gave Tibor's sister enough money to buy her own apartment in Hungary. His cousin Ágnes was also taken care of. Tibor also helped his nephew István, his sister's son, sort out the large problems with his teeth, of which he had very few in the front. Now with his new dentures he was a confident and a good looking young man. Every time he smiled Tibor felt really good inside. Jody and Bill too were nicely taken care of.

With the rest of the money they were making investments to fill the void created by his now non-existent salary and also do some fun things. Tibor has been able to invest into an up and coming rock band, managed by his good friend and ex-pilot colleague Martyn. They are called

Octane OK and they'd come a long way with Martyn's careful and skilful guidance. 2013 will prove a very important year for them all as they are about to release their debut album, recorded in Texas in the summer of 2012. The artwork was designed by no less than Storm Thorgerson!

When Storm suffered a massive stroke he was 58, Tibor's age at the time of writing this book. Although he survived the event, it very much influenced Tibor in the way that he takes care of himself today. He has never strayed from this path. When Richard died he was just 68 years old and for Tibor this really hit home as in just 12 years he would be that age. Apart from cycling and walking he goes to a gym twice a week, something he had always frowned upon - being in the fresh air had always been his thing. He loves the gym now and has become a demon at rowing. He works the weight machines, builds up a good sweat with a 20 minute swim at the end, rounding off with 10 minutes of Jacuzzi heaven! Libby keeps on working in her art studio creating her incredibly colourful pictures, does Yoga and they cycle and walk together often. She is equally as insistent in trying to stretch out her time on this Earth!

Chapter Twenty Four
The Present Day

As we already know Libby introduced Tibor to the family's holiday home in Blakeney early in their relationship. They have taken Tibor's sister Judit and her teenage daughter Virág with them there and they loved it. Sometimes they go with their business partners, Simon and Lucia. The business, which has been recently set up, is called Oxlip Developments Ltd. Tibor and Libby find them the easiest couple to get along with. They are both extremely cheerful, witty and charming. Simon is also the Chairman of the old January's family business, which was started many years ago by Libby's father Douglas. Douglas January was one of Cambridge's most well-known Estate Agents, Januarys. His wife Winifred, Libby's mother, always provided a lot of help with running the business. The company dealt with both private and commercial property transactions.

Derek was Douglas' business partner for a very long time and after Douglas died, in 1978 Derek took over the reins. Derek was highly successful in further developing the company to the extent that it has been able to provide all the family members with sufficient dividend income over the last 20 years or so. In later years the business has increasingly focused more on commercial property. When Simon joined the company alongside his father, Derek, there was an escalation in business and consequently in profits too. Tibor has always considered him to be something of a genius. On occasions he has been able to sit in on AGMs and has found Simon's presentations far from drab and boring, rather they've been funny and exciting.

Tibor and Libby in 2012

For these reasons they have set up their own business together. Tibor has always thought it would be absolutely amazing to be closely involved. Due to Derek's deteriorating health in recent years Simon has taken almost full control of running Douglas Investments (now Dernford

Holdings Ltd) and several other companies. As Tibor says, 'Simon's a real plate spinner!' Oxlip has just launched and is about to get started on their first project, a residential development. Tibor is very much looking forward to this and hopefully to many others to follow.

Epilogue

So Tibor's journey, which started from humble beginnings in Budapest in 1954 and where his passions for drumming and aviation were born, took him to Israel and, from guarding for the Israeli Army at Prison Six, to pursuing a musical career in London and finally propelling him into aviation. He rose to the very pinnacle in that world when he became the Captain of a Boeing 737. His life has been an extraordinary one - exciting, creative, rich and varied.

It has been my privilege to write Tibor's biography and I would like to tell the story of how this came about. I was giving a presentation of my work at Waterstones in Cambridge one evening in November 2012. Tibor and Libby graced the event with their presence. I was reading extracts from my novel *Nothing and Everywhere* and showing clips from my TV documentary *The Colours of Infinity*. The intention behind the event was to show the parallels between these two very different works as they both explore the power and wonders of fractals in general and the Mandelbrot set in particular. I was of course also promoting my novel. The presentation went well and afterwards Tibor came up to me and said how much he liked my writing and asked me if I would consider writing his biography. It was an honour to be asked and I said that I was most interested in principle to take on the project. We met again a month later and came to an agreement. I started the work before Christmas in the depths of the cold European winter and finished the writing in the tropical heat of the beautiful state of Kerala in southern India. You have just completed reading my offering and I sincerely hope that you enjoyed it and found me worthy of telling Tibor's impressive story.

Go to www.aerodrum.com
to visit Tibor's photo gallery and listen to his drumming.